first edition

# Get Rich Slow

## The *Truth*—Not The Hype— About What To Do With Your Money And Why

| first edition |

# Get Rich Slow

## The *Truth*—Not The Hype—About What To Do With Your Money And Why

**By Tama McAleese**
**Certified Financial Planner**

THE CAREER PRESS
62 BEVERLY RD.,
PO BOX 34
HAWTHORNE, NJ 07507
1-800-CAREER-1
201-427-0229 (OUTSIDE U.S.)
FAX: 201-427-2037

**GET RICH SLOW The Truth—Not The Hype—About What To Do With Your Money And Why**
ISBN 0-934829-71-3,   $8.95

Copies of this volume may be ordered by mail or phone directly from the publisher. To order by mail, please include price as noted above, $2.50 handling per order, plus $1.00 for each book ordered. Send to: The Career Press, 62 Beverly Rd., PO Box 34, Hawthorne, NJ  07507

Or call Toll-Free 1-800-CAREER-1 (in Canada: 201-427-0229) to order using your VISA or Mastercard or for information on all books available from The Career Press.

IMPORTANT: While much careful thought and depth of research have been devoted to the writing of this book, all content is to be viewed as general information only and should not be construed as actual legal, accounting or financial advice of a personal nature.

The ideas, suggestions and general concepts are subject to Federal, state and local laws and statutes. The ever-changing economic, political and international environment may well demand re-interpretation of some or all of the concepts presented herein.

The reader is urged to consult competent legal, accounting and tax advisors regarding all legal and personal financial decisions—This book is not meant to be utilized as a substitute for their advice.

| table of contents |

# Get Rich Slow

# Would You Rather Get *Poor* Slow?

It does not seem like a particularly good time to publish a book that actually seeks to impart practical, nononsense, common sense advice about managing your money: The American national anthem is "Shop until you drop." The average worker's idea of a retirement plan is winning the lottery. The big financial institutions are becoming wealthier every minute, even as they continue lending billions to Brazil and paying for Renoirs to hang on the chairman's office wall. And all of us are paying a bigger share than ever for all the programs Congress continues to legislate. We can't even trust the President's own lips!

Everyone is working *your* money for *their* benefit. Except you, of course. But then, if you *were* working your own money, you might actually have some left after everyone else got done with it. And then you might not need this book.

## Where's Everybody Running?

Two men on a hunting trip encountered an angry bear who did not take kindly to their trespassing. While the first man turned to run for the nearest tree, the second man sat down on a rock and began tightly tying his shoe-laces.

"What are you doing?" yelled the first man. "You can't outrun that bear."

"I don't *have* to outrun the *bear*," answered the second man. "All I have to do is outrun *you*."

Like our intrepid hunters, you are already well into the longest and most serious race of your life—protecting your hard-earned nest egg—and you're probably losing badly. Inflation is outpacing you, the financial industry is out-thinking and outmaneuvering you, the banks and insurance companies are outsmarting you, and the government is outvoting you and overtaxing you.

You've been lulled into a false sense of security, believing that someone else is dutifully standing guard over your hard-earned dollars and, thus, guaranteeing your financial future. In reality, you are painfully ill-equipped to outrun your adversary and ill-prepared to defend yourself against the big financial guns lined up against you. You might as well have showed up at the Shootout at the OK Corral with a squirt gun.

In the above story, the intended victim at least knew he was in serious danger and acted immediately to save his life. Real-life victims—the average American consumer—work hard for their money but fall almost as immediately for virtually every marketing gimmick designed to separate them from whatever they've managed to put away.

The problem is, most of you have never learned to play the Money Game.

## What's The Money Game?

The basic rules of the Game are simple. Either you work your money or someone else gladly will. The object is to grab as many dollars as possible in a limited amount of time. When the Game is over, the players with the most dollars, win. The losers go broke. They never develop an emergency fund, a college fund, a savings plan, or put away enough to retire in security and comfort. They probably *will* live long enough to outlive the small pile of cash they did manage to hide. And hope their *kids* have done well and are ready to support *them* for a change.

If this sounds easy, it is. If it sounds ruthless, ditto. But it is a true picture of where the average American is headed.

## And Why Are You Losing At It?

If the basic rules of the game are so simple, why are so many people playing it so poorly? Because the rules are in the fine print people don't even notice, let alone read—the small print on the contracts they sign, the monthly credit card statements they receive, the banking statements they throw into a drawer. They simply believe what they are told. They believe because they feel someone *some*where *must* be protecting them.

Most people are still searching for that elusive (and nonexistent) "free lunch," the winning lottery ticket that will solve all their financial problems. It is time-consuming and depressing to actual take control of their own financial lives—to read, to research, to scrimp and save...especially when everyone else *seems* (and that's the operative word) to be doing so much better with so much less effort.

Most people aren't planning to fail—they're simply failing to plan.

Sadly, too many Americans believe that a real financial planner or advisor only advises a client whether to buy stocks, bonds or some mutual funds.

So the average citizen independently continues to throw some money at financial goals, pick blindly from among a wide buffet of products, and cross his or her fingers. A very scientific way to ensure financial security!

When the financial goal becomes too close to ignore any longer, most people panic and respond immediately... by going deeper into debt. They console themselves with the thought that things will get better. Unfortunately, things tend to get worse.

I see far too many clients on the verge of a money crisis: Their child just turned sixteen. College is just around the corner. And they have *finally* figured out that the college fund (that was also the emergency fund *and* the savings account *and* the vacation fund *and* the Christmas Club) will stretch for six months...*if* the child never calls home, stays with strangers during holidays, and limits spending money to 44¢...per semester.

Six months before the first tuition payment is due is *not* the appropriate time to start planning for college. Retirement planning is nearly impossible if you wait until three months before you get your gold watch. Not even the best financial advisor can spin straw into gold. Or turn that gold watch into years of income.

And don't believe for one second that I'm talking about all those "other people" out there. Based on statistics, whether you or your friends would admit it or not, *most* folks are nearly broke. If most primary breadwinners lost their jobs for three months or more, they would lose their good credit record. If they remained unemployed for six months, their cars would be repossessed. If they couldn't find work within a year, they would most likely lose their mortgaged homes. Long-term financial planning in many homes consists of attempting to stretch *this* paycheck until the next one comes through the door.

You will probably not win the lottery. But, in your lifetime, you *will* make a small fortune. Americans are making more money than ever before. Why are they losing ground? Because it's not what you *make* that counts. It's what you *keep!*

## The Results Of Losing

If someone can talk you out of your dollar, that dollar is working for them. In ten years you will have only the fond memories of pizzas, designer clothes, and romantic vacations, while some stranger will have your dollars and have happily worked them for his or her own benefit.

Of course, there is always the government to give you a hand when you fail to take care of your own financial needs. But where will *they* get the money? It presently takes three workers to support one retiree on Social Security. Do some simple math—you will quickly realize that the government will be standing in the same soup line as you.

Let's remember that *we* are the government. It is *our* pockets that are continually picked for every program, subsidy, entitlement, or giveaway. The government *can* indeed give every one of us everything we desire. All we have to do is simply give the government all of our money, so they can redistribute it right back to chosen citizens (minus administrative costs, of course).

The goal of 1986's Reagan "tax reform" plan was to "level the playing field," to make sure everyone was playing by the same financial rules. How many of you are bringing home proportionally more than you did before 1987? Have you noticed that the more you make, the more Uncle Sam takes? Exactly whose playing field got leveled? Most middle-class Americans I know feel they lost some dirt along the way, dirt that showed up on someone else's field.

I have never attended a charity for anyone but the very poor. So if you manage to save a little, just not enough, you *will* be on your own. In this country, we don't let people starve just because they have mismanaged their money. If you manage to store away enough for your retirement, guess who is going to be at your front door, demanding you give some away?

## If I've Scared You To Death

I won't insult your intelligence by promising to send your children to college free, cut 80% of your current insurance premiums, show you how to buy real estate with "nothing down," or pretend that you can become rich without any risks. If anyone could actually produce those answers, do you think you could buy the information for $20? Or even $2,000? If so, this $8.95 book is a real bargain! (If anyone clearly had those answers, why would they tell *you?*)

*Get Rich Slow* is *not* going to solve your financial problems overnight. It is *not* some "Everything You Always Wanted To Know About Money" bible that will give you all the answers. *No one* knows all the answers, including me. But the average American isn't even asking the right *questions*.

If this book helps you at least do *that*—if it teaches you some healthy skepticism about the people who are so willing to "take care of your money" for you, if it puts you on the right track to save money for college, plan for retirement, live a better, more secure life—then it will have admirably served its purpose.

## Would You Rather Get Poor Quick?

This book was written out of the knowledge and frustration that this generation has a greater chance of starving to death *after* age 65 than of dying *before* retirement. As a Certified Financial Planner and longtime educator, most of the time I devote to my clients is spent repairing the costly mistakes they have already made.

Why did they make such mistakes? Because they were suckered (or suckered themselves) into listening to and believing *salespeople*—selling stocks, selling bonds, selling insurance, selling real estate—who, for the most part, owed greater allegiance to their own pocketbooks, their company's pocketbooks and their company's shareholders' pocketbooks (in that order) than they ever did to *my clients'* pocketbooks.

The financial markets—insurance companies, brokers, bankers, and the like—continue to produce anything they think they can convince you to buy—no matter how risky, how half-baked, how downright *dumb*—with the sure knowledge that many of you will believe them and buy it. Effective advertising and marketing blitzes use greed and fear tactics to encourage impulsive buying, leaving research and common sense far beyond.

Americans are whip-sawed from product to product and from company to company, never understanding what they have purchased or why. Each time they buy and sell—and my, don't they get advised to buy and sell a lot of different things?—a commission comes right off the top of their investment dollars.

If you became ill, you would probably visit a doctor and seek out his advice. If he became alarmed and advised you to go right to a hospital to have one or more popular parts of your body extracted, you would probably (and with good cause) seek a second opinion. Most people would do the same thing.

But these same people continue to perform self-taught surgery on their financial lives by giving away control of their money, implicitly trusting the self-styled financial gurus in their living rooms or on the telephone, never bothering to read the fine print in the contracts they purchase.

It doesn't take a rocket scientist to understand basic financial options. It *does* take some thinking and an understanding of the basic Money Game, the time value of money, the effects of inflation, the ability to read the fine print (and know what one is looking for), and some perspective on how all this dry theory actually works out here in the real world.

There are no magic pills that can provide uniform and simple answers to the many complex decisions you must make every day. Anyone who has worked for even a few years knows that it takes hard work to make money. To keep that money, save it, invest it, work it and profit from it will take some hard thinking.

The ideas presented here should make you skeptical, make you think, help you regain your common sense and apply it to control your financial life. This book the cornerstone on which you can build a solid financial future for you and your family.

## Or Get Rich Slow?

---

*Information is more valuable than money,* because with the right information and enough understanding of it, you can make good decisions and control your financial futures.

The problem is that it is nearly impossible to find objective, competent, and affordable advice. While the financial planning industry concentrates mainly on the affluent, high-income client, the rest of America is relegated to buying products they probably don't need and probably can't afford from salespeople who care about their own commissions far more than their clients' financial health.

Of course, there are always books. Unfortunately, most of the books I've seen are simply extended sales pitches— "Buy with no money down," "Get rich quick," "Get rich even quicker," "Get rich tomorrow!" and the like.

Today's consumer knows more about his car, his stereo, the plots of last night's TV sitcoms, and how to green up the lawn than he does about where his money is, who is taking care of it, and how well it is doing.

When a consumer buys a "lemon" of a car or a refrigerator, he soon discovers his mistake and either trades it in (so some *other* victim will have to suffer through it), throws it away, or yells loud enough to force the producer to replace it. But if he purchases a financial "lemon," he usually doesn't *know* it won't work until he actually *needs* it—at death, retirement, disability, the college age of his children, or during a medical catastrophe.

*Get Rich Slow* shoots from the hip and exposes those in the financial industry who are destroying your financial future. What you do with this information is up to you. But, if I am to give you the very best advice (and your money's worth), I cannot lie to you: You are being skinned with almost every financial move you make.

The Rockefellers and the Kennedys think of a dollar in different terms than the average American does. To middle America, one dollar can buy a burger, a lottery ticket to instant wealth, or a pair of shoelaces. To the affluent, that same dollar, carefully worked, will become ten dollars, a hundred, and, eventually, a thousand.

The wealthy know how to play the Money Game. The rich can *afford* some sloppy money management. The average consumer—you—cannot. The less money one has to work with, the harder that money must work.

## Whose Manure Is It, Anyway?

There was once a small bird who waited too long to migrate South. When it finally took off, it ran beak-first into an ice storm. Nearly frozen to death, it fell from the skies and into a barnyard. As it lay in the pasture, its heart barely beating, a cow passed by and deposited a coating of manure on top of it. This was a final cruel act, it seemed, given the little bird's already poor luck.

But the manure generated heat—warmth which acted like a blanket for the little creature. As the bird was warmed, its heart pumped more blood, the temperature rose throughout its body, and it began to recover. It was so happy to be alive it started to sing.

At which point the cat heard the commotion, found the bird, and ate it.

The moral: Not everyone who dumps manure on you is your enemy, and not everyone who pulls you out is your friend.

You must learn to separate your real friends from those whose *self*-interest is much stronger than any commitment to work in *your* best interest.

Do you remember the day you finally closed on your first home? You sat in the lending institution and signed away the next 20 or 30 years of your life as paper after paper was pushed in front of you. How many of those documents did you take the time to read through carefully? Probably none. There was no need. After all, you were deep inside the large and impressive protection of the institution where they kept the Big Money, with all those professionals helping you, with the real estate agent and your banker cheering for you to get over that five-yard line to the goal, like they were going to be part-owners right along with you. (How little you knew!)

Why, this was an everyday, mundane occurrence. There was no need for you to hold up everything at this critical point to read through all those documents you wouldn't have understood anyhow. Why bother to have a lawyer look anything over? *Their* lawyers already had, and *they* weren't complaining. Just sign, sign, sign. (Your physical presence wasn't even needed—only your pen arm needed to show up.)

Here was the sales and intimidation process at its finest. With so many professionals already "protecting" your interests, it seemed impudent and downright rude to actually ask someone what you were signing and to translate all the words you didn't understand. After all, there were other customers waiting their turns. Maybe you even felt the bank was doing you a *favor* by giving you the money you had so anxiously waited for. If they had this much confidence in you, how could you question their motives?

Yes, buying a home is a common, everyday occurrence. But so is delivering a baby, and, believe me, I remember every painful detail of both my blessed events. It is *not* a "common, everyday occurrence" to dish out every penny you've saved for a decade for a down payment. You don't sign away your life (and, perhaps, your firstborn) every day of the week.

With hearts pounding, eyes glazed and mouths closed, Americans go through the most serious financial transaction of their financial lives in the worst possible emotional condition for clear thinking and evaluation. Perhaps you survived without adverse effects, but many consumers do not.

## Let's Hand Out Some Grades

As a longtime educator, I know that if my classes are failing, I am failing, too. The financial industry has proven it is failing the consumer miserably.

The combination of greed and incompetence in financial services today is scary and inexcusable. Individuals posing as professionals in respectable advisory areas routinely and without guilt ravage middle America. Sound like Sherman on his "march through Georgia?" It could not be more deadly.

Instead of bullets and cannons, well-dressed and highly-trained salespersons calling themselves advisors, financial planners, counselors, or account executives and representing institutional names that symbolize credibility, routinely prey on the ignorance and naivete, as well as the basic laziness, of the middle class.

What's truly scary is that most of these salespeople will spend more of their time in company training classes learning to close a sale than gaining a thorough knowledge of the products they will offer. When I consistently understand financial vehicles better than the salespeople who originally sold them and made a commission on them, something is dreadfully wrong.

This book is not a scathing indictment of every advisor or counselor. It is intended to protect and prepare you so you can separate the frauds from the professionals, the empty promises in *bold* print from the real guarantees in *fine* print.

I hold out little hope of every changing the financial industry or of even wounding it in the heel. But I *can* hope that every one of you who picks up this book and reads even one chapter will have your financial life improved, will be better equipped to defend yourselves against the marauders of this industry, and will be able to realize at least some of your financial dreams and goals.

**Get Rich Slow** is a relatively short and "user-friendly" book for people like you who won't read financial books because they are long and boring.

It *does*, hopefully, convey a serious message: **Use it or lose it.** Either *you* work your money or someone else gladly will. But it then uses humor and common sense to help you create your armor—a financial action plan that will work for *you*. Simple forms and illustrations teach developing financial priorities and encourage commonsense thinking. Some chapters challenge traditional ideology. Some reinforce it. Some offer options you never knew you had.

You will find many ideas that challenge the beliefs you now hold. Myths and traditions are nice in December, but they didn't work for your parents, and they *won't* work for you—blindly follow the same ideas, and there is no reason to assume you will do any better than they did.

Financial planning concepts, money management techniques, and the time involved in learning to control and work your own money may sound boring, mundane and stodgy. If you agree, then this book is designed especially for you. It can be read in two evenings...or once a month for five minutes at a time for the next eight years.

Since at the end of eight years, this information won't do you as much good, I have written it in "plain English," and added anecdotes along the way to keep you going.

Good common sense is all it takes to win the Money Game. Two plus two should *always* equal four, even if some smart-aleck MBA attempts to convince you that the answer is only true in a base seven number system.

When you finish reading and studying this book, you will, perhaps for the first time, be equipped to go up against the "Big Boys"—the insurance companies, banks, brokerage firms, even the government—and win.

I dedicate this book to every one of my clients who persisted in following the rules outlined in it and gave me the reinforcement and encouragement to teach others how to control their financial destinies.

And to all of *you* who do likewise!

## chapter one

# The 12 Most Common Money Mistakes

Once upon a time there was a man of great faith who believed that God was an integral and vital part of his life. Every day he endeavored to live as he felt God desired.

The man lived in a small village next to a lazy river that irrigated the town's crops during the growing season. One spring the rains came, but instead of bringing new life to the fields, they turned into torrents, overflowed riverbanks, and threatened to sweep both buildings and people right to the ocean.

Most of the citizens quickly packed what they could carry and escaped in whatever transportation they could find, but the man of faith stayed behind, sneered at the menacing storm, and assured himself that God would save him, even as many of his neighbors implored him to leave.

As the water rose higher, the man was forced to ascend to a second-floor vantage point. As he peered out of his bedroom window, the villagers implored him to join them and leave while he could. They begged him to jump to safety. The man ignored them. He knew God would help him.

The water eventually rose so high that the man was forced to climb onto his roof. There he stood, his hands in the air, stretched towards the gray skies, waiting for salvation. Nothing happened. Only the last cries of the villagers beseeching him to save himself could be heard.

The man looked up to the heavens, clasped his hands above him, and yelled, "God, I have been faithful to You. I have lived according to Your laws and been grateful to You for all things. Why have You forgotten me now?"

There was a period of silence, then a thunderous answer from above. "My son," the voice rumbled, "Who do you think sent all those villagers and boats to save you?"

Many people depend only on faith and no planning for their financial futures. They optimistically assume that the bills will somehow get paid, their child will receive enough financial aid for college, and the government and their employer will come through with a comfortable retirement pension. Like the man who starved to death in a field, waiting for the roasted duck to fly into his open mouth, refusing to plan for the future is financial suicide.

Consumers tend to make similar financial mistakes. They pass on traditions that don't work and continue to believe propaganda which the financial industry churns out to take their dollars and work them for itself. The twelve mistakes in this chapter are the most destructive and sinister.

## 1. Live Now, Plan Later

Monetary dreams do not just happen. They must be well planned for. Things do not simply get better over time. On the contrary, they tend to become worse. Are you basically in better or worse shape financially than you were five years ago? Is your percentage of assets over debts increasing or decreasing? How have you planned to protect yourself against losing 6% (or more) of your yearly earnings to inflation? What are your contingency plans in case your company flies south with the geese next winter?

The achievement of financial goals does not depend on luck (sorry, lottery employees and administrators). It will depend on your using each chapter in this book and resolutely setting out to turn your life around and take control. Good intentions are worthless. Everyone has a reason why they didn't achieve greatness. Nobody will care why you didn't get to the top of your mountain. You simply must do it. If you have some interesting war stories to tell on your way up, then your biography will become even more interesting. You must learn to be a marathon runner. And you must start today.

## 2. The "Miss Scarlett" Approach

Individuals procrastinate. This is probably not the first money book you have read. What happened to the *last* set of good intentions to trim the budget, cut the consumer debt, and get started on a monthly disciplined plan to save? Let me guess. The next crisis came along, and you quickly returned to putting out one fire after another. Perhaps you talked yourself into a vacation, a new car, or an addition on the house, ridding yourself of any guilt by promising to start again on that darned savings plan...first thing tomorrow.

Maybe you decided you were young enough to have some fun first. You may have looked at your budget and concluded that next year's raise would be a better time to start saving. Christmas is certainly no time to start any compromising—we all know how important it is to support the retail stores so they don't suffer a recession. It is even possible that, once you took a good look at the financial hole you'd dug for yourself, you gave up altogether.

I have heard every excuse imaginable. The most creative was from a five-year-old, who told me he raided his piggy bank to get a toy he had been wanting because "he owed it to himself." Where do you think he heard *that* one?

## 3. Who's On First?

How do you budget your monthly income? What is the first bill you pay each month? What is the next? At the end of the month, what do you have left? Like millions of others, you probably have more *month* left at the end of the *money.* Before you pay for anything next month, put away something for yourself. Even $25 per month in a systematic savings plan will become a significant lump sum after just a few years.

If your parents were starving, could you buy $25 worth of food for them? Of course you could! Aren't you as valuable? Do you care as much for yourself and your family? Then you have the responsibility to pay yourself first. Think of that payment as a bill you owe to yourself. I can guarantee that in ten years the memory of bygone pizzas or entertainment will not be as valuable or keep you as warm as a significant nest egg for a new home, a college education, or your retirement.

Nearly everyone "fritters" away $25 per month. Once you start disciplining yourself, perhaps through a payroll deduction or automatic checking plan, you won't see the extra money and, therefore, you won't spend it.

## 4. No Problem. I Got A Pension

Workers depend on others for their financial security —Social Security, company pensions, insurance companies, lending institutions—and lose control of the use of their money. By turning over all of your savings to others, you deny yourself the basic decisions every person should make for him- or herself. No one watches your money like *you* watch your money. The savings & loan disaster surely proves that—would *you* have loaned billions of dollars to *Brazil?*

Few workers today still believe they are putting their Social Security payments into a fund account in their name. They know that money is going right down the street into someone's pocket for immediate use. How many of you believe Social Security will be there when *you* retire? Though projections state that, for a change, there is a surplus, they are simply "guesstimates," no matter how well-intentioned. Like bathrooms, everyone has one.

Let's put Social Security aside. If you get a little less than anticipated, you certainly won't starve. You've got your pension!

We used to believe that the responsibility of a company was to nurture and protect its employees. We are now beginning to understand the truth. If a company's profit margin can be made more attractive, it will move, leaving employees to fend for themselves. I have seen far too many 45-year-old workers (and executives) who have lost their jobs to ever believe in the sanctity of "company loyalty" again. That is not a great age at which to start over.

I think many people worry about whether their company will be in business *five* years from now, let alone at retirement. And, if it is, whether it will be able to pay out the promised pension benefits—some very large and well-known companies would show major losses if their future pension liabilities were added to their current balance sheets.

## 5. You Gotta Know The Rules

Consumers don't understand the basic rules of the Money Game. The magic of compound interest, the Rule of 72, the time value of money, and owning versus renting your own investments are critical strategies to your action plan. These ideas have been hidden from you by the financial industry for one good reason—they work!

The insurance industry has assets totaling nearly seven *trillion* dollars! How does that stack up against *your* assets? Whose money was used to create those astronomical figures? You loan institutions your money so they can invest it at a significant profit for themselves. How decent of you.

## 6. Custer's Last Command: Charge It!

Americans are caught in the "credit crunch." Everyone wants everything now. Neither governments nor individual families can borrow themselves into prosperity.

A credit card can be a valuable tool, like a hammer to a carpenter, if it is properly utilized. But if all you *have* is a hammer, sometimes everything looks like a nail.

Using "plastic" can establish a credit history for the time when you are ready to purchase a car or a home. It can allow you to use a company's money free for up to thirty days every month...if you pay off your monthly balances on time. It can also be an emergency card if your car needs towing or breaks down away from home. But it will be the greatest financial enemy you will ever know if it encourages you to feel richer, to live beyond your present means, and to fool yourself into believing you will be able to pay it off with future expected income.

The "credit crunch" is destroying lives because people are borrowing against their futures to support stratospheric consumption levels today. If you can't pay your credit card debt off in the next thirty days, you are spending too much. In fact, you are not *spending* at all. You are simply signing your name to a greater commitment to future obligations with money you don't have. If you cannot afford to pay off what you owe now, what in the world are you doing borrowing *more* plastic money?

It takes marketing genius to convince so many people to pay more and more for an item which becomes worth less and less as each day passes. The average consumer could care less how much his total debt is. He rarely even asks a salesperson. He simply asks the size of the monthly payments. How much will you pay for your car over the 48 or 60 months you have spread your payments? How many of your seed dollars will you fork over for your home? On a 20-year loan, over twice the amount originally borrowed. On a 30-year loan, over *three* times the original mortgage debt.

If *you* are getting deeper into debt, "plastic" surgery—cutting up all your credit cards—may be the only solution until you get back on your financial feet.

Most of us don't have a burning desire to leave a huge estate to our heirs at the expense of our own needs at retirement. But, since I know of no way to tell just how long each of us will be on this planet, we must plan on building up enough in reserve to see ourselves through. If we don't make it that long, I doubt we will spend our immortality wishing we had spent more and left less behind.

## 7. Look, Ma—No Hands

Effective advertising sells products. Corporations know that massive buildings, elegant environments, billion-dollar advertising blitzes, and catchy slogans impress you and create the illusion of stability, credibility and service, when, in reality, it's only the contract that counts.

A company attempts to create the illusion of friendliness to attract customers. When I hear or see commercials that blather on about a company's caring, understanding and "user-friendly" employees, I picture 5,000 or 10,000 people working with smiles pasted on their faces, their muscles in great pain, bending over backward to achieve their ultimate goal: "to serve and to protect."

I wonder how understanding these caring workers are when a customer misses a payment or, worse, falls totally apart at the financial seams. Perhaps those employees will continue to work hard, reassuring the client or customer that they understand this is only a temporary setback, and when he is back on top again, they would like to begin receiving the monthly payments once more. I can also fantasize that I will some-day win a Pulitzer prize. I doubt seriously the veracity of either assumption.

Slogans are carefully researched to deliver the precise emotional wallop necessary to whip you into a frenzy until you *buy that product.* In fact, I'll bet my next tuition payment that in 60 seconds you could recall at least a dozen advertising slogans, tunes or logos (trademarks) safely embedded in your brain and intended to part you from your cash.

In reality, companies are composed of highly stressed-out and ulcer-ridden management. They must confront constant change, competition from everywhere, the unexpected adversity of the marketplace, competitors constantly stealing clients and markets. And maintain a singular mercenary sense of purpose—to increase their profit margins. Stockholders are fickle, will sell at the first sign of financial trouble, and are constantly on the lookout for a hostile takeover.

If that isn't enough to make one run for the antacid, changes in interest rates, unpredictable economic cycles, and product obsolescence continually force marketing executives to create anything they believe they can sell to the public. Corporate games played inside a company's walls are ruthless. It is these dynamics, not altruistic principles, that drive corporations.

If your friendly neighborhood thrift or bank were on the verge of financial disaster and insolvency, would the president give you a call to advise you to pull out your deposits? If your investment company discovered that the accountant had absconded over the weekend with the entire year's profits, would you expect to receive immediate notice to withdraw your money before they declared bankruptcy? Would you be in line during a bank run to get your deposits before the money on hand was gone?

Unless you are the CEO's mother or brother, you are probably going to be one of the last to receive notice of bad news. Instead, you would be at work or at home, self-assured that you are in good hands with someone whose advertisements have made you feel secure.

## 8. Herman, You Need Better Glasses

Buyer's don't read the fine print. The old saying, "The bold print giveth, and the fine print taketh away," is still true. Every word in a contract you sign is important enough for the company's lawyer to have included it in the contract. It should be as important for you to understand how it will affect your financial situation. Too many people believe only what they are told. You must look further. There is no all-powerful winged avenger to watch over you.

Look at the following sentence: <u>I didn't say he stole that money</u> and how easily it can "read" differently:

<u>I</u> didn't say he stole that money.
I <u>didn't</u> say he stole that money.
I didn't <u>say</u> he stole that money.
I didn't say <u>he</u> stole that money.
I didn't say he <u>stole</u> that money.
I didn't say he stole <u>that</u> money.
I didn't say he stole that <u>money</u>.

By emphasizing or deemphasizing different words, I have made the same sentence imply seven entirely different meanings.

## 9. No Kidding? A 45% Return And No Risk?

Optimists believe unrealistic promises and extraordinary expectations of return. If it sounds too good to be true, it probably is. Remember: No one is ever going to pay you any more than they must to induce you to hand over your fist full of dollars. Not the U.S. Government, not private industry, and not your neighborhood lending institution. The more they pay you, the less they have left. This is just common sense.

When you listen to promises that you are going to become a millionaire, you are setting yourself up for a big disappointment. Many products today increase the yield they promise by increasing the risk to the consumer.

If it looks like a duck, walks like a duck, and quacks a great deal, chances are it is still the same old bird dressed up in a brand new set of feathers.

## 10. My Deductible is *$100,000* ?

Policyholders don't understand self-defense risk management (buying insurance protection) and the most cost-effective methods for getting the greatest value for every dollar spent. Most have the wrong types of insurance in the wrong amounts and are paying too much for what they have. Should you protect your assets or your liabilities? The answer to that question is vital to your pocketbook and to your family.

If the major breadwinner died tomorrow, the average family would likely be broke within one or two years. At the same time, people are "insurance poor" because they are paying too much for the coverage they do have. The average life insurance policy death benefit last year was under $7,000 due to borrowing against cash values and the high cost per unit of coverage. How far will *that* take a wife and children?

When an agent intentionally under-insures a family because his commissions are larger on some other products, he makes a conscious decision to deliver a small check to the funeral home. There should be something illegal about that, but there isn't.

Did you ever hear of a widow who gave away part of her husband's death proceeds because she thought she had too much? No one ever asks at a funeral how much the insurance policy cost. All that is truly important is the size of the death benefit check.

The insurance industry has spent 150 years tightening up its contracts and honing the marketing strategies designed to get your signature on the bottom line. Consequently, marketing is what they do best. It's too bad that product quality at a reduced cost isn't at the top of their priority list. Consumers can be led into products that do little for *their* pocketbook but very nice for their agent's.

Too many agents don't tell the whole truth, especially on newly-designed products which are confusing and potentially misleading, because there are no laws that force them to. Do you know what you have? What you have bought is not what you have been told but exactly what your policy contract states, and I *know* you can't read that.

## 11. Who's Ahead—You Or The IRS?

People purchase products for the wrong reasons. This puts their savings in these products at risk. What are the most popular words these days? Tax-deductible, tax-deferred, and tax-exempt. Everyone knows what they mean because they are magic marketing techniques. But most people have no idea of the underlying investments and how well they will work.

I once sat in a Chicago seminar with an industry "professional" who showed my group how to use those magic words to get the client to demand that an agent sell her two products instead of one because the proposition sounded so good. Not once did this "professional" mention the nature of the underlying vehicle. A potential buyer could have been investing in gun-running, drug smuggling, or research on the breeding habits of goldfish and not have known what she was buying!

Far too many consumers buy tax-exempt or tax-deferred products which don't work as well as a taxable investment could. Folks misunderstand the role of tax shelters and do not become involved enough with their own tax situations. With more tax loopholes closed every year, it is vital you learn what remaining strategies can reduce your tax bite. After all, your money can do more good around your house than around Uncle Sam's. Purchasing small handbooks by authorities will help tame the insatiable tax beast.

Every wage earner has a tax problem. The average worker works 2 1/2 hours each day for Uncle Sam. You will work approximately 80,000 hours before you retire. Are you working for a living or for a life?

Tax planning does not begin on April 1—it begins on January 1 of the *previous* year, while there are still viable strategies to keep more of your income.

## 12. Your Mother Should Know... But Probably Doesn't

Generations pass on traditions which do NOT work. The last generation didn't drink or gamble their money away. Where it did go? They simply gave it to others who smiled and said comforting things, like "trust me." They were kept in the dark like so many mushrooms and fed a steady diet of propaganda.

How well have our revered financial institutions served the older generation? The only elderly retiring in comfort are those who watched over their own money, understood money principles, and made their money work harder than inflation through the years. Ignoring the effects of inflation on fixed income vehicles and settling for less than a 50-50 partnership with those who use your money are pathways straight to slow starvation after retirement.

## 13. What Is That Newfangled Investment?

(Baker's dozen.) Investors utilize outmoded vehicles and give up flexibility and liquidity to move as their financial lives change. In my opinion, no one's money should be resting sleepily in a passbook savings account, working at a rate less than the rate of inflation. With so many options today, it is ridiculous to let your money depreciate and erode.

Don't expect your *banker* to suggest you move to a better-paying vehicle and increase *your* profit at *his* expense. Banks loan out money based on the time deposits they can count on. The more money they have tied up, the more loans they can make. It is *not* in their vested interest to offer you their best deal if you are voluntarily willing to settle for less.

With seven-day CDs, NOW accounts and money market mutual funds, even your short-term cash can be earning competitive rates. Moving your money from something paying you 5% to one paying 9% a year amounts to an 80% annual increase in your yield. Banks also have sales on money, and smart consumers shop for interest rates like they do for linens and groceries.

But don't change just for the sake of change. Before you jump into an attractive-looking product, ask what hidden costs are involved if you change your mind in six months, one year or even five years. Many products have severe penalties for withdrawing—with deferred charges, back-loaded expense charges, early distribution charges, and pre-retirement penalties.

You certainly want a competitive return (though not at the expense of control and flexibility) as your personal goals and the economic environment change over time. You *can* depend on a salesperson to bring up every *positive* aspect of a product. You can*not* depend on him or her to cut his or her own throat by revealing every *disadvantage* that may talk you right out of the sale.

Which reminds me of a story. (As you continue to read this book, you will soon see that a number of mundane financial discussions remind me of stories. It's one way to keep you going!)

A long time ago a king was auditioning court jesters. One candidate came forward and announced to the king that he could, within one year, teach the king's horse to talk. Obviously, everyone was astonished. The king immediately vested the candidate with the title of Court Jester and gave him and his assistant a beautiful room in the castle, fine food and drink, and access to all the pleasures of his Kingdom.

As the new jester and his associate left the throne room, the assistant whispered to him that he, too, was astonished to find that his friend could accomplish such an unusual feat.

The jester just smiled. "A year has 365 days and nights; each day has 24 hours," he explained. "A lot can happen in so many hours. The king could die. I could die. The horse could die. The kingdom could be lost in a battle. And, who knows, the doggone horse might even learn to talk. In the meantime, we have a nice life for a year!"

Make sure any promises made in the heat of a sale are backed up on paper. Are you sure *you* would never fall for a "talking horse?"

## chapter two

# Financial Foreplay

---

**T**he first step to achieving anything valuable is to institute a plan of action. Whether you are planning a revolution, the entrapment of your favorite guy or girl (or someone else's guy or girl), or a defense worthy of an Oscar when that state patrolman stops you for speeding, every goal needs a fail-safe plan of action.

Financial planning is no different. Most people already have a financial plan. It's stored away casually in their heads. And it sounds something like this:

*We would like to buy a house sometime in the future—can't save up much now because I don't make very much yet—besides we need that vacation this summer away from the kids...*

*And speaking of kids, they have been pestering us to get a pool like the Millers' next door...*

*The car has been acting up lately. I really need a new one, with air conditioning...*

*Sure, we want the kids to go to college—I think we'll be all right on that one—I can start to save in a couple of years. Besides Joey is pretty smart— he'll probably get a scholarship...*

*Retirement? Oh, I'm all set—my company has a pension plan, and I have Social Security. After the kids are out of college, I should be able to start to save some extra for retirement—since the house will be paid off, we'll be rolling in bucks...*

*If I'm laid off? I've got unemployment and a few bucks saved up—should be enough—besides I can always get a job with my brother-in-law if I want...*

*If I get sick? The company has some kind of health policy on me, and my wife can always work if we need the extra income. Right now, it's all we can do to keep ahead of the bills—the credit cards, you know—they can sure add up before you know it. We just got another one so we have plenty of credit, if we need it...*

*I'm sure things will get better and then we'll be able to save for the future.*

## The Time Value Of Money

Assume your goal at age 65 is to accumulate a lump sum of $100,000, and you expect you can earn 10% a year on any money you invest.

If you start at age 25, you will need to contribute only $16 per month.

Wait until age 35 to start saving, and you will need to fork out $44 per month.

Starting at age 45 will cost you $131 per month.

If you follow the most common retirement plan, you will wait until you're 55, at which point you'll have to sock away $484 per month. (See the chart on page 30.)

The same rate of return over longer periods of time makes the difference. By letting time and compound interest do most of the work for you, you can achieve your $100,000 goal much more easily and with less money. Maybe you're not 25 any longer—wait much longer, and your problem will get even larger, your goal even more unreachable. The time to start saving is always NOW!

## RETIREMENT GOAL OF $100,000 AT AGE 65

| Age | Needed/Month | Rate of Return | | Value At 65 |
|-----|-----|-----|-----|-----|
| 25 | $16 | 10% for 40 years | = | $100,000 |
| 35 | $44 | 10% for 30 years | = | $100,000 |
| 45 | $131 | 10% for 20 years | = | $100,000 |
| 55 | $484 | 10 % for 10 years | = | $100,000 |

The enemy of any plan, financial or otherwise, is procrastination. (There was once a town so full of procrastinators, they vowed to start a procrastination club—naturally they never got around to it.) By systematically setting aside even a small amount of money each week, each payday, or each month, over time you will have accumulated a significant nest egg. If you let yourself be talked out of your money, that egg will be hatching in someone else's nest.

## The Plan! The Plan!

Developing a financial plan involves shutting off the TV (you may have to pull the plug) for at least one night and having a family council. Use your discretion whether to include your older children. If they will work with you as part of a team, this will be a big help, as they should be taught basic money management skills, too.

It may also be helpful for you to once more reinforce in their selective memories that you are not a tree with money growing out of your ears, and that you are going to an early grave attempting to support them in the manner to which they have become accustomed. Using fear, tempered with subtle doses of guilt, may produce a valuable exchange of ideas which can be pooled. If this is out of the question, due to unpleasant earlier experiences, at least work with your spouse to develop your financial plan.

Through experience I have found that the first session occasionally revolves around one of two basic themes:

1) *He has made all the money, and he gives her his entire paycheck, which he never sees again, while she spends every lousy cent and then some, which is totally the reason they are in this sad financial shape at present;* or

2) *She has tried 1,151 recipes to disguise hamburger as fish, quail, or even mousse, and she can't remember the last time she got a new dress, possibly when she promised her husband she would have a baby boy and he bought her a full maternity wardrobe.*

The above roles may be reversed, but the script is usually the same. If you feel that no valuable benefit can come from the two of you being left alone at this point, either bring in a stranger who abhors violence and can't be blamed for favoring either side, or use a financial planner as a mediator.

A spending plan or budget doesn't *prevent* you from getting what you want. It *helps* you get what you want.

It does not *take* time. It *saves* time.

And to save you even more time, I have included two checklists—"How To Successfully Complete Your Financial Plan" and "How To Successfully Develop A Working Monthly Budget" on pp. 46-49. Refer to these checklists as you follow the steps through the rest of this chapter.

## Congress Has It Easier, You Claim?

Start with the Goals, Objectives & Attitudes Worksheets on pp. 50-53. Based on your family discussions, decide what is important to you right now and what isn't.

Then write down all your specific objectives under each of the major categories—retirement, estate, educational, income and other.

Then fill in all the blanks in the Attitudes section.

Together, these two sections form the basis for the rest of your planning.

Decide what the family's most important short-term goals and long-term goals are. Short-term goals may include establishing an emergency fund, reducing consumer debt, or financing college (especially if it's just around the corner). Long-term goals may be adding to retirement savings, starting a college fund, beginning a small business, or purchasing a new home.

For a single parent this planning becomes even more vital—there is only one breadwinner. Make your goals more specific than "keeping your head above water", "staying above the national poverty level," or "becoming filthy rich."

The next step—the very basis of any financial plan—is a cash flow statement, which will actually show you, once and for all, what money is coming *in* and how much of it is going *out* and *to whom.*

Creating an environmental plan to save the ozone may be easier than coercing most people to actually write down their monthly expenses. It is time-consuming. It is boring. It is going to be depressing—we already know that. *It is also the most necessary part of your entire plan!*

If you proceed without this step, you are figuratively tying your shoelaces together before attempting to run a four-minute mile. You must see the real numbers on a piece of paper in front of you to really understand your current financial position. And until you know where you are, there's no way to figure out how to get where you'd like to be.

Look at the fill-in-the-blanks "Monthly Cash Flow Statement" on pp. 54 and 55. At the very top is a line for

Net Take-Home Pay. This figure should be your monthly income and based on a regular workweek, *not* including overtime *unless you can depend on that overtime month after month.* Pull out your pay stub or employer earnings statement and use the figure from a normal workweek.

If you are paid weekly, multiply your weekly paycheck by 4.3 (weeks per month). If you are paid every two weeks, divide your semi-weekly paycheck by 2, then multiply by 4.3.

Do *not* use your gross income figure—this is not the amount you actually have to manage; it is only what your employer told you he was going to pay you the last time you got a raise.

Next, go through each expense category and write down what you spend on each per month—as realistically as possible. Utilities, for example, vary each month. Average the bills from winter, which are the highest of the year. The idea is to avoid the juggling act each month because there is not enough money to pay everything that comes due. Even though every expense is not paid month- ly, the money will be in the checking or savings account until it is needed, and in the meantime, it can be working in an interest-bearing account for you. Items such as clothing, entertainment, car maintenance and house maintenance are more difficult to estimate. Be as realistic as you can. When in doubt, estimate *higher.*

A new car will require less upkeep that an older one, but tires, oil changes and other incidentals will still add up each year. Older vehicles need water pumps, temper- ature gauges and radiators.

Clothing for children tends to increase that category's totals. Shoes, winter coats and a new dress or suit will expand those expenses. If you review last year's charge card statements, you should get a rough idea of the miscellaneous clothing expenses that have increased your borrowing and debt levels. You should budget for those items, and pay for them with cash.

Not all bills will be paid on a monthly basis. Auto and homeowner insurance premiums, real estate taxes and medical expenses may only be paid on a semi-annual or annual basis. Even though the money physically does not leave your account monthly, divide the payment due by the number of months the payment will cover. For example, semi-annual property taxes should be divided by six so that money will be accumulated by the time the actual payment is due. In the meantime, it will be working for you, and you will not have to juggle that expense at the last minute.

There is no category for Christmas. Most people overspend too heavily in this area and take nine months to pay off presents from the previous year. Children need a college fund more than the latest toy or designer jeans. Decide beforehand on a maximum limit and either set aside money each month for the following holiday or purchase your gifts out of "miscellaneous" throughout the year.

Though Christmas clubs usually pay an abysmal interest rate, I would recommend them for those who find it impossible to systematically put away Christmas money out of current spending reach. At least this will act as a temporary way station—cash that is not easily available until the holidays arrive.

Total all monthly expenses and put that amount at the top of the page after "Net Outflows."

Subtract your net expenses from your monthly income.

Most clients are amazed when they compare the amount of money coming in to the amount of expenses going out. There is usually a large amount of money missing, what I call "fritter" money. Fritter money is unconsciously spent, does little long-term good, and must be recaptured and put aside for savings, college or other future goals, such as retirement. A significant portion of this should be put at the top of your monthly expenses, and it should be the first bill you pay each month. This is one bill you pay to yourself.

It can increase your emergency fund, start a college fund, or add to retirement goals. It is not as important what vehicle (savings account or credit union) is utilized at this point. The main idea is to put something away each and every month. As your income increases and your debt level decreases, increase the monthly savings payment.

Occasionally, the difference between what comes in and what goes out is a minus number—you are spending more than you make, month-in, month-out. This requires immediate attention and extra effort to plan how to reduce those expenses as quickly as possible. Borrowing is not the answer. That "easy" solution is how you got to this point in the first place.

Plan with today's income and do not use expected future income in your calculations. Attempt to stay within the general percentage allowance for each category of expenses listed on p. 54: If possible, the first 10% of net income should flow into savings of some type. The mortgage (including property taxes and homeowner insurance) or rent should be kept to no more than 22% of take-home pay. Consumer debt (including car payments) must be kept under 18%. Disposable income expenses (food, clothing, utilities and other costs to keep you alive and comfortable but that do not purchase anything tangible which can appreciate over time) will likely require 50% of your income, especially if you have children.

It may be necessary to throw in any overtime pay so as not to destroy any confidence you might have built up for this project. Add in the value of next month's grocery coupons, any coins you may find under the furniture cushions and the current recycling value of aluminum from pop cans, whether they have been opened or not, which you can sell for salvage.

Once the cash flow statement has been completed, look at each area and star any category that can be reduced. Insurance premiums—auto, homeowner and life—can be reduced simply by shopping for more competitive rates. Though some overhead expenses are fixed (mortgage or

rent payments, utilities, gasoline and food) other areas
can be at least marginally decreased (telephone, clothing,
vacations, entertainment and miscellaneous).

## Putting Your Budget To Work

What is the first bill you pay each month? If you
answered the mortgage or rent, think again. The first bill
you pay is to Uncle Sam, who takes your money and redis-
tributes it to strangers. You can be more mercenary and
establish an IRA, an employer qualified plan at work, or
even a Keogh if you are self-employed.

How do you budget each month? Most folks pay bills in
the following order: the mortgage or rent first, then utility
bills, car payments, food, and last, a scramble to afford the
monthly minimums on credit cards, time payments, and
miscellaneous expenses. Medical bills usually go to the
bottom of next month's pile because we all know that doctors are filthy rich and they couldn't *possibly* need their
money as badly as we do at this moment.

Let's try a different approach to monthly budgeting.
Assuming that you have found some small light between
what comes in and what must go out, pay yourself first.
Even if you can't save 10% of your net income—the
amount I recommend as a target—saving *some*thing now
is vital. Paying yourself first is the most underrated way to
accumulate wealth over time.

The second bill is now the mortgage or rent. Then, as
you prioritize them, come all other necessary expenses.
What we have done here, simply by "paying ourselves
first," is recover some of the "fritter money" from the bottom and move it to the top.

Paying yourself first will force you to become more
frugal with your spending habits because the other bills
must be paid. With that extra money, you can immediately begin stashing money in your new emergency fund.

An emergency fund is a special account which can be used for unexpected bills which may arise. It should be built up to at least 10% of your annual net income. If you are a seasonal employee (such as construction or other uneven employment), you should have a back-up fund of at least three months your annual net income.

Once you have built up a reasonable emergency fund, do not be discouraged that it dwindles down. Emergencies *do* arise. And that *is* the purpose of the fund: to provide money for items you previously bought on credit or at the expense of your other financial goals. Keep putting money into this fund on a regular basis. Eventually, you will reach a level that is comfortable for you. Then you can begin to attack your long-term goals by reallocating that monthly payment to another investment goal.

You must learn not to juggle your finances from month to month—paying the mortgage this month, the utility bills the following month, and the doctor bills when the notices become more frequent and hostile.

## Last But Not Least

Finally, list your assets—long-term savings, Series EE bonds, employee retirement plans, other securities, etc.— on the Portfolio Planning Worksheet on pp. 56 & 57.

If these pages remain nearly blank, funnelling money into one of these areas should be a priority. Keep this record and add to it over time. It will give you a quick and complete estimate of your net worth now and in the future.

Income taxes have not been included in this process because they are taken out before you receive your take-home pay. If you are receiving a large refund after tax season, then you are giving an interest-free loan for an entire year to the U.S. Government and . At the end of the tax year, Uncle Sam gives it back to you (with no interest, of course).

Could I make this kind of deal with you? How about giving *me* an extra $75 or $100 per month (before you ever see your own paycheck) so I can work it for my own benefit and give it back to you with no interest in April of the following year? The most common justification is that if the money were available, it would be spent on nonsense during the year. At least this way there is a check in one lump sum that can be used for some beneficial purpose.

If you are using this method as a forced savings accumulation, establish a monthly amount that you are overpaying in federal taxes and have it withdrawn from your paycheck and transferred into some type of weekly or monthly investment for your use. Then you will have your money working throughout the year for you. It will be withdrawn from before it gets to you, you won't see it, and, therefore, you won't spend it foolishly.

Reduce your deductions at work so that you receive no more than $200 or $300 back after the tax year. Be careful not to be too generous to yourself—if you wind up owing Uncle Sam money, you will be penalized.

## Planning Never Ends

Having completed your financial plan and committed both checklists to memory, it is vital that any major expenditure be in line with your new budget. A face-lift may not get a majority vote at this time, and the annual hunting trip with the boys to stalk bear at a favorite garbage dump may be out for another year.

Put your budget up on the refrigerator so it can be seen daily. It will be a good reminder of the commitment your family has made. Don't be afraid if friends drop in and discover it. They will probably be relieved to find out you aren't doing any better than they are. Now that everything is out in the open, they can spend less money to impress you and start on a savings program themselves.

Review your plan at least once a month. Hold another family council to pass around the credit (or attach blame). Attempt to make each member of the family responsible for some part of the plan's success. For example, if your teenager has decreased the number of times she has called a casual friend in Venezuela, you will want to offer some positive reinforcement.

Make up your mind to stick to the plan. Reevaluate it from time to time if it can be improved. If temporary emergencies occur which make the plan impossible to continue, start it again as soon as possible. (Emergencies do NOT include getting your hair bleached so you can be seen again in public or buying a new lunch pail for work because your son was learning to use a hammer and nails and you are now consigned to using his lunchbox with a decal of Teenage Mutant Ninja Turtles on it.

The most important point is to use your money wisely. When you have mastered control over your everyday financial life, you will feel a real sense of accomplishment and self-satisfaction. Once you are on your way, the rest of your attitudes about money will change, and you will begin to view money in a new light. Use the following forms and get started.

# HOW TO SUCCESSFULLY COMPLETE YOUR FINANCIAL PLAN

1. Decide to start today.

2. Include at least your spouse in your discussions.

3. Fill out the basic goal and objectives worksheet.

4. Don't attach blame—there is probably enough for everyone to share.

5. Fill out *completely* the monthly cash flow statement (budget worksheet).

6. Group items in the following categories: 1) savings and investments; 2) home mortgage or rental expenses; 3) consumer debt; and 4) disposable income expenses.

7. Star those areas which can be reduced (such as insurance premiums, utilities, entertainment, vacations, consumer spending, etc.)

8. Compare net *(not gross)* take-home pay to outgoing monthly expenses.

9. Take the necessary steps to balance the budget. Someone may need to temporarily bring home extra income.

# HOW TO SUCCESSFULLY COMPLETE YOUR FINANCIAL PLAN

10. Put your budget on the refrigerator where it can be seen and followed.

11. Immediately develop a back-up emergency fund.

12. Start a monthly systematic savings plan.

13. Negotiate monetary rewards occasionally to reduce financial stress.

14. If you suffer temporary budget overflows, start again as soon as possible.

15. Work on debt management at the same time that you develop the emergency fund.

16. Don't become too zealous in paying off consumer debt at the expense of developing a savings plan.

17. Even a small amount each month should be saved. As income and other financial burdens improve, increase savings.

18. Cut your consumer debt; if necessary, cut the credit cards.

19. Turn your finances around patiently. Look for signs of progress.

# HOW TO SUCCESSFULLY DEVELOP A WORKING MONTHLY BUDGET

1.  Calculate monthly expenses for all listed categories on the Cash Flow Statement.

2.  Estimate variable outflows such as utilities, clothing, and car and home maintenance.

3.  Divide occasional bills such as taxes and insurance premiums into monthly payments.

4.  Utilize a strategy for accumulating Christmas funds.

5.  Examine all categories to reduce outgoing expenses (e.g., auto, homeowner, and life insurance, entertainment, and miscellaneous.

6.  Total all expenses and list in the "Net Outflow" space.

7.  Calculate all dependable net income. (For weekly paychecks multiply 4.3 weeks per month for accuracy.) Try not to include overtime.

8.  List all net income in the space "Net Take-Home Pay."

9.  Pay yourself first.

# HOW TO SUCCESSFULLY DEVELOP A WORKING MONTHLY BUDGET

10. Pay all other bills in order of their priority.

11. Keep remaining money due for future payments in an interest-bearing account temporarily.

12. Develop an emergency fund.

13. Remember what the word "emergency" means.

14. Compile current assets on the Portfolio Planning Worksheet.

15. Reduce overpayments on federal taxes by increasing deductions.

16. Sign up for an automatic payroll or checking deduction plan to transfer that income for future financial goals.

17. Discuss and negotiate every major capital expenditure.

18. Keep the budget handy and in full view as a reminder and commitment.

19. Stick to your plan—reevaluate it over time.

# GOALS, OBJECTIVES & ATTITUDES
# WORKSHEET

Date: _____

List all your objectives under the following major categories—the more specific the better:

Retirement: _____

_____

_____

_____

_____

_____

_____

_____

Estate Planning: _____

_____

_____

_____

_____

_____

_____

_____

Educational: _____

_____

_____

_____

_____

_____

_____

_____

Income (Is there a need for current monthly income?):

_____

_____

_____

_____

_____

_____

Other: _____

_____

_____

_____

_____

# ATTITUDE CHECK

1. Rank above objectives in order of priority.
2. Target overall after-tax return per year: _____
   (If all bank deposits, figure 5.77%; if some growth vehicles, figure 9%.)
3. Expected inflation rate: __ (Industry generally predicts 6% per year.)
4. Would you alter your current lifestyle to attain your objectives?
5. How active do you want to be in managing your investments? (Note: Individual stocks, bonds, and other issues require active management.)
   ❑ Very active ❑ Somewhat active
   ❑ Not very active ❑ Inactive

6. Define short-term objectives (less than 2 years):

_____

_____

_____

_____

_____

_____

_____

_____

7. Define long-term objectives (more than 2 years):

_____

_____

_____

_____

_____

8. How much risk can you (or are you willing to) tolerate?

❑ A lot ❑ A fair amount ❑ Not a little, not a lot
❑ A little ❑ As little as possible

9. Are there areas you would *not* consider for financial objectives?

❑ Yes ❑ No

If so, what? _____

_____

_____

13. Please rank the following in order of their importance to you:

___ 1) Financial provisions for family/spouse (in case of death)

___ 2) Retirement income needs for yourself/spouse

___ 3) Educational plans

___ 4) Special plans or objectives

# MONTHLY CASH FLOW STATEMENT

Monthly Take-Home Pay

Monthly Expenses:

Fritter Money (Take-Home Pay
Minus Outflow):

2264

1447.14

816.86

## Monthly Expense Detail

10%  Savings and Investments: _____

Include company pension plans, individual retirement plans (IRA's, Keogh's, etc.), establishing an
emergency fund and general investment accounts

22%  Housing Costs
Monthly Mortgage Payment/Rent : _410.00_
Property Taxes (per month): _____
Property Insurance(per month): _____
Home Equity Loan Payments: _____

18%  Consumer Debt
Dept. Store Accounts: _____
Credit Card Accounts: _200.00_
Bank Loans: _____
Car Payment(s): _385.14_
Other Time Payments: _____

50%  Other Monthly Expenses
*Child Support/Alimony: _____
*Electricity: _30.00_
*Heat: _____
*Telephone: _25.00_

*Water: _____
*Auto Insurance: 137.00
*Life Insurance: _____
*Medical/Dental: _____
*Other Insurance: _____
*Groceries: 150.00
*Gasoline/Diesel: 80.00
*Car Maintenance: 30.00
*Entertainment: _____
*Cable TV: _____
*Clothing: _____
*Vacation: _____
*School Tuition: _____
*School Supplies: _____
*Organization Dues: _____
*Subscriptions: _____
*Household Items: _____
*Miscellaneous: _____

Total: _____

*This area may have to be slashed to allow for savings and investments and overruns in other areas. If monies used for "other monthly expenses" represent *less* than 50% of total take-home pay, other areas can be expanded—e.g., purchasing a bigger home or increasing the savings and investing portion.

## Present Lump Sum Obligations

Mortgage Balance: _____
College Tuition: _____
Other: _____

# PORTFOLIO PLANNING WORKSHEET

Primary Investment Objective:_____

_____

_____

1. Cash, Checking Accounts, Emergency Funds, CDs

| Where Deposited | Objective | $ Value | Percent of Portfolio |
|---|---|---|---|
| _____ | _____ | _____ | _____ |
| _____ | _____ | _____ | _____ |
| _____ | _____ | _____ | _____ |
| _____ | _____ | _____ | _____ |
| _____ | _____ | _____ | _____ |
| _____ | _____ | _____ | _____ |
| _____ | _____ | _____ | _____ |
| _____ | _____ | _____ | _____ |
| _____ | _____ | _____ | _____ |
| _____ | _____ | _____ | _____ |
| TOTAL | | _____ | 100.00% |

2. Retirement Programs, College Funding, Vehicles For Other Goals:

| Name of Vehicle | Objective | $ Value | Percent of Portfolio |
|---|---|---|---|
| ___ | ___ | ___ | ___ |
| ___ | ___ | ___ | ___ |
| ___ | ___ | ___ | ___ |
| ___ | ___ | ___ | ___ |
| ___ | ___ | ___ | ___ |
| ___ | ___ | ___ | ___ |
| ___ | ___ | ___ | ___ |

3. Regular Investment Programs (IRA, SEP, 401K, 403B, profit-sharing, ESOP, bonds):

| Name of Vehicle | Amount of Investment | Frequency | Present Value |
|---|---|---|---|
| ___ | ___ | ___ | ___ |
| ___ | ___ | ___ | ___ |
| ___ | ___ | ___ | ___ |
| ___ | ___ | ___ | ___ |
| ___ | ___ | ___ | ___ |
| ___ | ___ | ___ | ___ |
| ___ | ___ | ___ | ___ |

| chapter three |

# Get Interested In Interest

Just about everybody can figure out that the higher the rate of return (interest) you receive on your money, the faster it will grow. But how fast is "fast?" And how can you predict what you will actually have at any given time?

*The Rule of 72* is a ballpark method of determining how fast money will grow at any interest rate. Just divide the number 72 by the rate of return you are receiving. The answer is how many years it will take to double your money. The following examples should help:

At *3%* per year, your money will double every 24 years (72/3 = 24)

At *6%* per year, your money will double every 12 years (72/6 = 12)

At *8%* per year, your money will double every 9 years

At *9%* per year, your money will double every 8 years

At *12%* per year, your money will double every 6 years

Always use the number 72. I don't know why tornadoes only head for trailer parks. And I don't know why to use 72 instead of, say, 92 or 52. I *do* know that it is a fairly accurate and simple way to compute return.

Let's examine how this principle applies to real dollars. As an example, I have figured the interest on a $2,000 investment (a typical IRA contribution). Taxes were not considered for this illustration, and the money was contributed at the beginning of the first year.

| Contribution | $2,000 | $2,000 | $2,000 | $2,000 |
|---|---|---|---|---|
| Percent return | 6% | 8% | 9% | 12% |
| After 12 yrs | $4,024 | $ 5,036 | $5,625 | $ 7,792 |
| After 24 yrs | $8,098 | $12,682 | $15,822 | $30,357 |

Two points are critical. First, the higher the interest rate, the larger the account value over time. More importantly, doubling the interest rate *more than doubles* the return over longer periods of time. Look at the 6% and the 12% columns. After 13 years, the difference between the 6% and the 12% yields is more than double. And the gap continues to widen—at the 24-year mark, there is a difference of almost four times the return between the 6% and 12% investments.

Now let's see what happens to your money when you loan it out to others. According to the Rule of 72, at 15%, money doubles every 4.9 years. At 20%, money will double in 3.8 years.

| | Your Return | Their Return | |
|---|---|---|---|
| | $2,000 @ 6% | @ 15% | @20% |
| 12 years | $4,024 | $10,701 | $17,832 |
| 24 years | $8,098 | $57,250 | $158,994 |

If you feel this comparison is unfair because no one could *possibly* be making that kind of return on your money, check out your credit cards and finance company rates—some of those are even *higher.* So don't be so ready to stick your savings in a passbook savings account and slowly pay off your credit cards—the difference over time between what you're getting and what your paying is tremendous!

Now that you understand how important the Rule of 72 is to your financial future, strive to get the highest return on both short-term and long-term savings. The Money Game teaches one very sobering lesson: *Use it or lose it.*

## When Time is Money

Albert Einstein was once asked to describe his most notable discovery. His answer: "Compound interest. The miracle and magic of compound interest."

Whether or not the above story is true, he's right. The businessman most familiar with compound interest is not the CEO of a large conglomerate or a corporate accountant working daily with cash flow charts. It is the grocery store owner in your community. Poor man. His markup on shelf items is usually only one-half of one percent per sale. Most large corporations would have become extinct ages ago with such a piddling profit margin.

But how long does that can of soup or bottle of milk stay on the shelf? The store owner may make only a tiny profit per item, but he does it over and over in a relatively short amount of time, and each time the profits are converted into new inventory for sale.

Because of constraints on space, personnel and limited markets, no store owner can increase profits infinitely. But your money has only *two* basic constraints: The rate of return you receive and the amount of time the money can work for you until it is needed. If you give your money enough time to work and the most competitive rates of return you can find, it will produce the miracle you will need to fund whatever you desire. You can have it all; you just can't have it all *today*.

How powerful a concept is this? Consider the man who applied for a job and was given two options: He could receive $300 per week for one month's employment or a penny the first day, two cents the second day, four the third, eight the fourth, and so on for for 30 days. Which option would *you* choose?

A penny may not seem like much in comparison to $300 (which is, after all, 30,000 pennies), but the magic of compounding can make it powerful, indeed. If you took the penny and the deal, at the end of 30 days you would have *$5,368,709.* Try working it out yourself.

Of course, no real employer would offer such a deal. But it effectively illustrates the advantages of compounding even the smallest amount of money over time.

Here's another example of the power of compound interest over time—the story of two twins, Bill and Bob. When both were 24, Bill decided to take care of his retirement and invested $2,000 a year in an IRA account at the beginning of each year. He received an annual rate of 10% on his investment, and he continued to religiously contribute to his IRA for the next five years. Then he stopped. He never added another penny to his retirement account.

Bob, however, was more interested in fast cars and an even faster lifestyle. He saved nothing for the first six years. But as he grew older, he began to worry more about retirement. So at age 30 (just when Bill *stopped* contributing to his IRA), he began to put away $2,000 per year into an IRA account at 10% return per year.

By retirement at age 65, each twin had accumulated more than $450,000. This nest egg cost Bob only $12,000, but Bill was forced to invest $2,000 for 33 years—*a total of $66,000*—to accomplish the same goal. Would you rather spend $12,000 or $66,000 to make $450,000?

|  | Bill's Investment | Bob's Investment |
|---|---|---|
| Age 24 | 2,000 | 0 |
| 25 | 2,000 | 0 |
| 26 | 2,000 | 0 |
| 27 | 2,000 | 0 |
| 28 | 2,000 | 0 |
| 29 | 2,000 | 0 |
| 30 | 0 | 2,000 |
| 31 | 0 | 2,000 |
| 32 | 0 | 2,000 |
| 33 | 0 | 2,000 |
| 34 | 0 | 2,000 |
| 35 | 0 | 2,000 |
| 36 | 0 | 2,000 |
| 37 | 0 | 2,000 |
| 38 | 0 | 2,000 |
| 39 | 0 | 2,000 |
| 40 | 0 | 2,000 |
| 41 | 0 | 2,000 |
| 42 | 0 | 2,000 |
| 43 | 0 | 2,000 |
| 44 | 0 | 2,000 |
| 45 | 0 | 2,000 |
| 46 | 0 | 2,000 |
| 47 | 0 | 2,000 |
| 48 | 0 | 2,000 |
| 49 | 0 | 2,000 |
| 50 | 0 | 2,000 |
| 51 | 0 | 2,000 |
| 52 | 0 | 2,000 |
| 53 | 0 | 2,000 |
| 54 | 0 | 2,000 |
| 55 | 0 | 2,000 |

|  | Bill's Investment | Bob's Investment |
|---|---|---|
| Age 56 | 0 | 2,000 |
| 57 | 0 | 2,000 |
| 58 | 0 | 2,000 |
| 59 | 0 | 2,000 |
| 60 | 0 | 2,000 |
| 61 | 0 | 2,000 |
| 62 | 0 | 2,000 |
| Total investment | $12,000 | $66,000 |
| Amount at age 65 | $477,020 | $591,633 |

Perhaps you are muttering to yourself that this concept is great for your children, but it comes too late to keep the wolf from your door. The concept remains the same, whether you are 5, 35 or 55. The only difference is that the less time you have, the harder your money must work. Since your time is limited, you have no time to lose.

Sit down tonight and explain the story of Bill and Bob to your children. That may even be a better idea than sending them to medical or law school. It's too late for us adults to use time as effectively as our children can because the longer money can work, the greater the future lump sum will be. It seems to gain momentum like a snowball rolling downhill.

Einstein's theory of relativity may have great benefits to science, but in the race to beat inflation and provide those dreams and goals you have promised yourself and your family, the theory of compound interest has greater "relativity."

## Inflation: The Silent But Deadly Money Killer

If I told you that, as one of my best clients, I would offer you a special investment opportunity that was worth $1,000 in 1945, had steadily declined in value each and every year since then, and was now selling at $320, would you purchase it? That is what inflation has done to the American dollar! Because inflation erodes money away quietly, it is largely ignored by the consumer but certainly not by institutions and corporations who use your savings or lend you money.

*Webster's* has a lofty definition of inflation: "An increase in the currency circulation or a marked expansion of credit, resulting in a fall in currency value and a sharp rise in prices." Phooey! Inflation is *not* some boring theory of interest only to economists. It represents a *real loss*.

I once owned the most lovable and obedient pup, but Ralph had one major problem. He was terrified of larger dogs. Every time an aggressive canine headed toward him, instead of running for safety, he sat down, turned his head, and pretended not to see the aggressor. The end of this story is obvious. He was often bitten from behind.

Ignoring inflation is a serious mistake, much like turning your back on an aggressive pooch. If inflation is trotting along at 6% per year, you must *earn* 6% *(after taxes)* on your money *just to stay in the same place you were at the beginning of the year.* If inflation is *greater* than 6%, you must receive an even higher return just to continue treading water.

Let's look at the effect of inflation on savings. Assume you have $10,000 working at 6% interest with a 6% inflation factor working against you.

---

### How Inflation Hurts You

| | |
|---:|:---|
| $10,000 | Savings at beginning of year |
| 600 | Interest @ 6% (before taxes) |
| —168 | Taxes on interest (28% bracket) |
| —600 | Inflationary loss of money (6%) |
| 9,832 | Real purchasing power at end of year |
| 168 | Total loss in one year |

Carry these losses long enough and the bottom line will become zero. The longer your money works below inflation, the more seed money you will use up. Each year you will gain less interest, because there is less money to receive interest on. If you're an elderly couple needing to live on the income your seed money generates, it's easy to see why you are having problems.

The effect of inflation on wages is even more unsettling. If it takes $30,000 per year today to keep your family and home going, in ten years at 6% inflation you will need $53,725 per year to retain the same purchasing power. In 20 years it will cost you $96,214 per year. Where are you going to find that kind of money?Are you going to get those kinds of raises at work?

Whether you are young or old, you must beat inflation with your future retirement money. It is imperative that you seek higher interest returns and growth of your long-term money. Some people are so frightened to move out of anything that is not guaranteed that they are actually incurring losses after inflation is considered. Of all the guarantees you may hear about, the one no one advertises is the guaranteed *loss* which you alone may sustain. Fixed income vehicles have NOT generally kept pace with inflation over time.

Inflation is more deadly to your financial health than high blood pressure or heart disease is to your physical health—nothing can cure the ravages of inflation after its symptoms appear. Americans have seen their savings insidiously eroded since 1970 at an unbelievable rate.

## My Daughter The Doctor

In my lectures, I always include the effects of inflation on higher education, and young couples immediately start thinking about limiting the size of their families. A good public university currently costs about $6,000 a year. That won't keep your kid in pizzas, but it will pack enough educational skills into him or her so that he or she can ultimately find another source of revenue other than blood-letting you.

Present college costs are escalating at 8% to 10% per year. But let's ignore reality for a moment and assume education expenses will increase at just 6% each year.

If Debbie is starting college next year, your total cost for four years will be $26,248. You'll have to lay out $37,233 for 12-year old Bruce. And cute 6-year-old Zelda will cost you $52,815. No wonder she smiles a lot. She knows she's going to do some sales job to coerce you into handing over *that* much money. (Maybe she has also seen your college fund languishing away at 6%.)

If you are debating whether to add one more child to your cozy family, future college costs may change your mind. Can you lay your hands on an extra $74,920? That's the projected price tag of college in the year 2010. For that kind of money you would think you could have the school named after you (or at least a gymnasium). And, of course, we have been talking about state universities. If the Ivy League is your goal, you may need to double or even triple these numbers. (See Chapter 11 for a more detailed discussion of college funding.)

## A Rose May Be A Rose, But 8% Is Not Always 8%

Financial institutions realize that many consumers have finally learned to search for the highest interest rates on their savings and investment dollars. So interest rates at many banks and S&Ls (the ones still in business) are more attractive than ever. You can even receive competitive rates on short-term deposits. That's the good news.

But they also realize that most customers have no idea how to use the concept of compound interest to compute the best annual yields, especially if they go out of their way to confuse you by using different ways of figuring interest (simple vs. compound) combined with different periods (semi-annually, quarterly, monthly. Money market mutual funds may even compound daily).

Is a 9.5% yield for nine months better than a 10% return for twelve? How about a 6-month deposit at 8.75% vs. a 7-day CD yielding 8.95%? By mixing interest rates with a variety of maturities, institutions can baffle the savviest customer.

There is, for example, a new marketing technique that is bringing in billions of dollars to a number of banks. Here's the ad you usually see: "Six-Month CD at 7.75%!"

What a great return in six months! If you're getting 7.75% for only six months, that's the equivalent of 15.5% for one year. Nobody I know is getting that great a return on a CD. What a deal!

Unfortunately, as we've seen, if it sounds too good to be true, it probably is. The 7.75% interest the bank is touting would be paid to you if you left your money in a CD for a whole year. But you're not. You're buying a six-month (half-year) CD. *Ergo,* your yield is one-half of that advertised rate: 3.875%. This is nowhere close to the most competitive rate for CDs out there. You've lost.

You can be sure of two things. No one—not your bank, not a large corporation, not your insurance company, and certainly not the U.S. government,—is going to offer to pay you any more for the use of your money than they absolutely have to. We can also assume that they will also charge a borrower (you) as much as *they* can to allow you to use "their" money.

Deposit $10,000 into a passbook savings account earning 5% at your local bank and you will fall asleep watching it compound. Now borrow that same $10,000, from the same bank, and you will be looking at 10% interest or more ...compounded in a different manner. You work your money at 5%. They work it at 10%. Considering that it may be your very own money that you are borrowing, that's some partnership!

Since compound interest works best the more frequently the money is compounded, let's analyze the effect of various compounding on a lump sum with an advertised rate of return of 8%.

---

### $10,000 @ 8% for 1 year

| | | |
|---|---|---|
| Simple interest | = | $800 profit |
| Compounded semi-annually | = | $816 profit |
| Compounded quarterly | = | $824 profit |
| Compounded monthly | = | $830 profit |
| Compounded daily | = | $833 profit |

---

You can immediately see that the *more often* the money is compounded, the *greater* the profit over a specific time period. Over longer periods of time, this relatively small difference will provide a much larger nest egg.

As long as you know the annual yield and how often the money is compounded, you can calculate the annual *effective* yield and compare rates. This is essential given the many strange ways banks, brokers and insurance companies advertise the return they are supposedly offering you, as it will allow you to actually compare apples to apples (or lemons to lemons).

For those of you who fear that anything remotely resembling a calculator is, by definition, not user-friendly, there is an easier method. Before giving your money to any institution, ask the smiling respresentative one simple question: "If I put my money in your hands for one year, how much profit will I have at the end?" Compare his or her answer with those of at least two other institutions.

If the representative cannot give you an answer, ask to see the manager. If he or she cannot quickly calculate an accurate response, run with your money out the front door as fast as you can. Any novice with the cheapest calculator can figure out the answer. Do you really want to leave your hard-earned dollars in a place where they can't even calculate compound interest?

I'd hate to think that every time they conducted a transaction they had to count it out on their fingers and toes in the back room. Of course, they have computers that do all the work. Is that supposed to make you feel more comfortable?

Financial institutions know the customer is willing to shop around at first but soon gets tired of watching his or her money. Some institutions advertise great yields on short-term CDs, knowing that after one or two weeks, those high advertised rates will drop right through the floor.

Although it is impossible to continually move your deposits as interest rates change from place to place (you would lose your profits to telephone calls and gasoline, not to mention losing your insanity), I advise clients to check short-term rates every month with their institution. If you feel you can do better, move your money. Lenders need the stability of time deposits to loan out money on a long-term basis. If enough customers show resolve in this area, companies will stop playing these games.

Just remember: *Without you, they'd have no money to lend!* So find a lender that is willing to respect you. And respect can be easily defined: Whoever offers you the best return on your money respects you the most. Financial institutions may have begun to understand they must compete for your money, but don't expect them to comply freely or to not try to confuse you in the bargain.

This is serious business: Every fraction of a percent you forego now will decrease your future dollars. If the institutions make poor decisions, poor loans (remember the S&Ls?), or mismanage assets, there are government entities which will indemnify them (or find ways to get us to indemnify them through increased taxes).

Who will cover the losses *you* suffer because you mismanaged your own portfolio?

| chapter four |

# Card Games With A Fixed Deck

Imagine for a moment that you could purchase only one item at a time through credit. You could buy *nothing* else (except with cash) until you had finished paying for the previously charged item. What would you purchase first?

If you answered your home, how would you get to work every day?

If you said your car, where would you live? You would have to rent for a long time. And by the time the car was paid off, it would be time to buy a new car again.

How would you ever afford a home? What about Christmas presents, clothes, vacations, pools, furniture, appliances, hospital and doctor bills?

Is it difficult to imagine your lifestyle without credit?

Is it impossible to imagine *any* form of life without it?

## Those Nice Credit Card People

The credit card is the financial industry's drug for everyone who just can't manage to stretch that paycheck as far as their high-flown lifestyle. And it's so convenient!

Buy now, pay later. Buy a *lot* now, pay just a *little*...for a lot longer. Live life to the fullest. You deserve it. Why wait? You could be gone tomorrow.

Before you consider nominating credit card companies for a "Humanitarian of the Year" award, let's take a closer look at whose doing what to whom (you): Credit cards, according to the companies that issue them, are their permission to buy something you really *don't need* right now at a price you really *can't afford* right now with money you *don't have* right now. Does this make you think they may have a hidden agenda?

## I'm Buying Tahiti. Here's My Amex.

I am the parent of one medical student and one law student. Neither possess any visible means of support, except for their two parents who are struggling and digging early graves to support two pricey colleges. The net worth of both would fit on the head of a pin.

Guess how many credit cards each has? My daughter has five, one of which now boasts a $7,000 limit due, of course, to her (!) splendid payment record (which is, needless to say, *my* payment record). My son has four.

I have *no* cards with a $7,000 limit, and I can whip up a pretty convincing net worth statement when I have to.

As graduate students living "poor and in debt," they could conceivably use their credit cards to buy a small town out West, or at least a small palm-dotted island in the Pacific.

I congratulate the credit industry for being so farsighted. Not satisfied with the unconscionable prices they charge adults for money, they have already begun on the next generation to insure the industry's longevity and to make sure our children understand the virtues of living in debt. If the credit industry can hook our kids while they are young, they can keep them dependent on borrowed money forever.

# What Do *You* Owe?

The average consumer really doesn't know how much in debt he is...and is probably scared stiff to find out. He only understands the size of each monthly payment. The more outstanding debt you buy (you are really buying money at a price), the more it will affect your future goals. A high debt level can affect the next five to ten years of your life. You will pay high monthly payments to a lender instead of to yourself. An astronomical debt level can lead to long-term disaster.

As we saw when filling our financial plan, the consumer debt of the average family—which includes car payments, credit card loans, time loans and other obligations (items bought on credit, but not including your home)—should consist of *no more than 18% of your take-home pay.*

And young couples with two working partners should *not* include both paychecks in determining the 18% figure (the *consumer debt ratio*). If the couple had a baby and the wife left the work force, the sudden drop in income—combined with the imminent additional financial responsibility of a new baby—would turn almost any family's financial stability upside-down.

You don't have to be poor or middle class to overextend yourself. I remember one young professional couple who together were earning more than $70,000 a year. They came to me because they were *spending* $80,000 a year.

The only realistic solution to their dilemma was to drastically cut the level of debt. Because they could not discipline themselves to cut their own spending, I advised them to cut up all their credit cards and simply start paying cash for anything they needed or wanted.

When they arrived at my office, credit cards in hand, the husband looked like he was going into cardiac arrest, and the wife's face was tear-streaked. This was the most painful act they could remember!

But they did it. They bought their freedom that day—financial freedom that would eventually allow them to reach their future goals and dreams. It felt so painful because they had come to depend on satisfying every comfort. Their present lifestyle was destroying their future.

## But I'm Paying Every Month!

If *your* consumer debt level is greater than 18% of your take-home pay, you must start to trim it immediately. Continuing to pay only monthly minimum payments endears you only to the credit companies, *because many cards are designed **never** to pay off as long as you continue to use them.* In fact, some companies' minimum monthly required payments are less than the interest due for that month.

For example, assume your minimum payment this month is $20.00. If you looked at the interest column, you'd discover that this month's interest is $25.00. If you pay only the required minimum payment, there will be an extra $5.00 of interest left unpaid. This $5.00 will be added to next month's balance, which will charge you interest on the loan *and* on that unpaid $5.00.

With *this* type of payment schedule, you will sink deeper into debt over time, even though you stop charging and continue your payments. You could conceivably pay on this type of credit card for 20 years, *never* charge again, and watch the unpaid balance *increase* each month.

The best customers, in the eyes of the credit card companies, are the ones who are loyal buyers, never pay cash, and pay the minimum each and every month.

I can guarantee you an 18% to 20% return on your money simply by getting you to pay off your credit cards. Where else can you get that kind of risk-free and tax-free return?

## Gimmicks And Gadgets

Presuming you're not ready to pay everything off tomorrow, how can you avoid some of the games the credit card companies play, even get them to play by *your* rules?

If you didn't feel compelled to do so in chapter 2, now's the time to make a list of all your credit cards and monthly installment loans or obligations. Include appliances, your car(s), and anything else you have bought on installment payments, excluding any home equity loans. (Use the form on p. 81.)

This will enable you to find out, once and for all, what you are really paying for the privilege of buying now, paying later, and losing all along the way. Rest assured: If there is a marketing gimmick in one column (such as an abnormally low interest charge), the credit card company will find a way to make up its loss in another column (the annual fee or the way they *compute* the interest). Fill out all the columns and then compare each card with the others.

How do the credit card companies fool you?

## 1.5% X 12 = 19.561%?

The ***annual percentage rate (APR)*** on your credit card statement is derived by multiplying the monthly interest rate by 12 (months in a year). For example, if the monthly interest rate is 1.5%, the annual percentage rate is 18%. But this is not a *real* number, at least not to you and your money. It's credit card company arithmetic—if you carry a balance on a card over an entire year, you will pay *more* than 18% for the use of the borrowed money.

How could that be? Let's examine what happened to the interest you paid during that year. Each month, after crediting your payment, the company charges 1.5% on the remaining balance. The following month another 1.5% is charged on the remaining balance. At the end of the first year, due to the effects of *monthly compounding,* you really paid 19.561%, not the 18% *simple interest* you have been led to believe. Compound interest, in this case, works *against* you.

The APR is designed to convince you that you are paying 18% *simple* interest on the borrowed money when, in truth, you are really paying 1.5% monthly *compound* interest. A little more "truth in lending" is in order here.

## Hey, Our Card Is Free!

Most credit cards also charge you an annual fee for the privilege of overspending. Some don't. Are these bargains? Not necessarily. A company which charges no annual fee may have higher interest rates (APR). Some companies advertise no annual fee for six months or a year, then tack one on in your monthly statement when the initial period is finished.

How are you supposed to know that? They told you in the original contract you received when you were approved, or they sent you a disclosure in your monthly statement, that piece of paper with words so small that an amoeba would have a hard time reading the print.

The smaller the print, the harder you have to work to read the message. So you throw it away (just as the credit card company hoped you would), and tell yourself it must not be important.

## And Only .0001% Interest!!

A company that advertises an attractively low initial interest rate may already be planning to raise that rate in two or three months. It *knows* you don't keep track of the small changes on your statements and that it will be several months (if ever) before you even figure out that you are paying more.

The credit card companies know who and what they're dealing with: The same shoppers who would fight for a 75¢ coupon dropped on the supermarket floor ignore the *dollars* that are being extracted right before their eyes.

Some very low interest credit cards charge from the point of sale (from the moment you purchase your item), and have no grace period whatsoever. By the time you receive your bill at the end of the month, you already owe some interest. You will never use these companies' money free for even one minute.

Most major credit cards charge on a variable interest scale. Heads you lose, tails you lose. If interest rates spike, you suffer an *immediate* interest hike. Of course, if interest rates *drop,* it takes substantially longer for the average institution to drop its monthly rate.

And be careful with cash advances—the interest clock generally starts ticking *from the moment you receive the money,* not from your closing date or the date you receive your monthly statement.

Companies realize the average consumer is not a persistent animal. Though he may make a half-hearted attempt to make his money work harder for him, they know that he will eventually fade like the fabled rabbit that was outwitted by the wily turtle.

(Please note that while this author has compared credit card company game plans to the famous turtle, she does *not* suggest that credit card companies are even remotely like turtles.)

## You *Still* Believe Lunch Is Free?

Another pitfall to avoid is what I call the "free from monthly payment" ploy. At Christmas, when you are pressed to find money to buy presents for a host of people you didn't talk to during the year, it becomes more difficult to continue with a monthly schedule of budgeted payments. Just in the (Saint) nick of time, the credit card company comes to your rescue, which proves it, too, has a big heart.

After all, it's the holidays, and they understand you want to get your little one that extra doll or train. Therefore, you are allowed to miss the regularly scheduled monthly payment. What a relief! You now have an extra $50 or $75 or more, which you run right out and spend (on their credit card, they pray) because, for some reason, you just feel richer.

Don't kid yourselves: The credit card company didn't stop computing interest during that time. They just held off sending you the unfriendly computer message warning you that you didn't pay last month and they had better see your check pretty darned soon. Your *following* month's bill comes with a larger interest payment stuck to it. Neat trick!

Here's another danger: When your credit limit is raised—and they always do it just as you reach your previous limit, don't they?—you feel like they gave you an A$^+$ on a test. You are proud that you are a valued customer, and you feel an increased sense of pride (and wealth).

This sales technique, along with your (assumed) lack of self-discipline, will simply create higher debt levels. If you couldn't pay off the original debt, why are you adding more? And if the same company is stupid enough to offer a student with no means of support a $7,000 credit limit, why would you want to do business with them anyway?

Another credit card company tactic involves marketing insurance, securities, CDs, and other financial products through their monthly statements. ***Never buy financial products from a credit card statement.*** You have *no* idea what you are getting, and, even if you call the given "800" number for more information, most people don't know the right questions to ask.

If you sign a contract or enter into one by telephone credit card, you are liable for the promises contained in the credit agreement. Ignorance is usually not a good defense against your greed. It is your responsibility to research before buying. If that deal on paper looks too good, it probably is.

## The $15 Phone Call

Many credit card companies will happily sell you credit card protection against theft or loss for as little as $15 a year. The company (after notice from you) will contact every company that's given you a credit card so you will not be liable for any fraudulent debts from unauthorized use. How do they know where you have credit cards? *You* have to make up a list and send it to them for their files.

This is a scare sell, as you are only liable for $50.00 on most cards *even if you never notify them* (which they told you in the original credit brochure, but, then, you probably didn't read it, did you?). Besides, you can maintain the list yourself, can't you? (See p. 80.) And if your wallet is stolen or lost, you can simply call the same toll-free numbers.

The $15 you save by doing it yourself is enough for one large pizza and drinks, a bottle of good wine, a movie for a family of three, or nearly two copies of this book, which could be given to your friends.

## Hey, Guys. Let's Play *My* Game.

If you intend to use other people's money (OPM) religiously, without paying any interest charges, look for credit cards with no annual fee, even if the APR is 30%.

What do you care? You will be paying off the card every month, playing by *your* set of rules and with *their* money.

If, however, you are in the habit of overbuying and paying monthly bills on credit, then look for the lowest interest rate you can find and forget about the annual fee.

If you purchase a combination of both large and small items, some of which can be paid off each month, then look for one of each of the above types of cards.

How many credit cards should you have? That all depends on your buying habits and your self-discipline. Two major credit cards are sufficient to provide for all contingencies. If you own a business, it should have its own set of credit cards so you can keep business and personal expenses separate.

The *more* debt you have, the *fewer* cards you should own. Credit can become obsessive. If you do not have a candy bar lying around, it becomes more difficult to add those extra pounds. The same is true for credit cards.

If you are paying on installments, list your card fees and APRs (annual percentage rates), target the highest interest rates, and throw more money at those balances. Pay down the lower interest rate cards at the monthly minimum. The total amounts you owe on each do not matter in this case. It is the *percent* of monthly interest you are paying that really counts.

Do not get so zealous in this area that you forget to build up your emergency fund. The money you are funnelling into freedom from debt won't help much if you find yourself short of cash in an emergency. Then you will need to draw a cash advance, where interest starts from the moment you borrow the money, and you will be back in the credit hole again. Dig yourself out systematically.

Remember, when you borrow Other People's Money, compound interest works against you. The only way to defend yourself and thwart *their* game strategy is to pay off those cards as soon as you can and start using their money free each month.

Issuers won't notice your new strategy, but in a few months, you certainly will.

# CREDIT CARD REGISTER RECORD

| Card Issuer | Card Number | Phone Number |
|---|---|---|
| | | |
| | | |
| | | |
| | | |
| | | |
| | | |
| | | |
| | | |
| | | |
| | | |
| | | |
| | | |
| | | |
| | | |
| | | |
| | | |
| | | |

# CREDIT CARD COMPARISON SHEET

| Issuer | Amount Owed | APR | Annual Fee |
|--------|-------------|-----|------------|
|        |             |     |            |
|        |             |     |            |
|        |             |     |            |
|        |             |     |            |
|        |             |     |            |
|        |             |     |            |
|        |             |     |            |
|        |             |     |            |
|        |             |     |            |
|        |             |     |            |
|        |             |     |            |
|        |             |     |            |
|        |             |     |            |
|        |             |     |            |
|        |             |     |            |
|        |             |     |            |
|        |             |     |            |

## THE DANGER SIGNALS OF DEBT

1. You don't know how much consumer debt you owe, and you're afraid to add it up.

2. You hide the bills from your spouse until a "good time."

3. You pay only the minimum or less (!) each month.

4. You juggle other bills to keep up minimum monthly payments.

5. You've reached the credit limits on *all* your cards.

6. You borrow for items you once bought with cash.

7. The portion of your income used to pay debts is rising.

8. You are increasing debt based on expected income increases.

9. You no longer contribute to a savings account, or you have no savings.

10. You are usually late paying some or all of your bills.

11. *This* month's credit balances are consistently higher than *last* month's.

12. You borrow money to pay for regular household expenses.

13. You borrowed money from a new source to pay an older overdue debt.

# THE DANGER SIGNALS OF DEBT

14. You applied for more credit cards to increase borrowing.

15. In the past year you have significantly increased your credit cards.

16. You have drawn from savings to pay regular bills.

17. You don't have an emergency fund to cover three to six months' expenses.

18. Your emergency fund is less than your short-term debt.

19. Creditors are sending overdue notices.

20. You pay your bills with money earmarked for other financial goals.

21. More than 18% of your after-tax income goes for consumer debt.

22. You postdate checks so they won't bounce.

23. You hurry to the bank on payday to cover checks already written.

24. You use cash advances from one card to make payments on others.

25. You *think* life without credit cards seems unthinkable.

26. You *know* life without *any* kind of credit is unspeakable.

# A CREDIT CARD CHECKLIST

1. Check the annual percentage rate (APR) on purchases and determine how it is calculated.

2. Check whether the APR is fixed or variable; if currently fixed, check whether it can be changed later.

3. Check whether the company charges a minimum finance charge no matter how small the unpaid balance.

4. Are there fees for each transaction?

5. What is the fee charged for each cash advance?

6. What is the APR for cash advances? Is it higher than the interest rate for regular purchases?

7. What are the late payment fees?

8. What does the company charge for over-the-limit purchases?

9. Is there a grace period? If so, how long?

10. How does the company determine the monthly account balance on which it levies an interest charge? How is your monthly payment split between cash advance balances and purchase balances? (If payments are apportioned between the two, it will be impossible for you to pay off your cash advances in full until *all* of your purchases are paid in full.)

11. Compare annual fees, and pay off all balances each month. Otherwise, opt for cards with the lowest annual percentage rate.

12. If you have a no-fee card, review your agreement to be sure the company will not levy one later...when they think you aren't looking.

13. You may be required to take a cash advance as a condition of membership. Read all the fine print... carefully.

## chapter five

# Insurance 101: Let's Explode Some Myths

If you could buy only *one* type of insurance, which policy do you think you would most likely need?

1) Life insurance;

2) Major medical or hospital expense;

3) Homeowner's

4) Auto insurance;

5) Credit life or mortgage debt protection;

6) Disability income.

Survey says: Disability.

If you are under 65, the likelihood of your being disabled for thirteen weeks or longer is greater than dying, losing your home by fire, suffering a catastrophic medical loss, having a major auto accident, or needing home mortgage insurance to pay off the debt.

Disability income was probably *not* your answer.

Why?

Because no one teaches consumers how to assess risk, how to purchase the correct kinds and amounts of insurance that you do need, and what kinds of insurance you *don't* need (or don't need *as much* of).

## Spreading The Risk

There *are* basic rules for managing risk and choosing the best values for your insurance dollars. Since risk is everywhere, you can respond in several ways.

First, you can *avoid* risk. Most people resist any temptation to free-fall from an airplane, but it is nearly impossible to avoid traveling in a car. Some risks can be easily avoided. Others cannot.

Second, you can *reduce* risk. Everyone has been through some "close calls." Most of you made immediate resolutions to be more careful. This is risk reduction, as is keeping equipment in good repair, eliminating cigarettes from your lives, installing smoke detectors and security systems, wearing auto safety belts, and driving defensively.

Third, you can *retain* it. This means to actually *keep* the risk, to insure *yourself.* That may sound inadvisable since you thought you were buying insurance precisely to protect you from such risks. But that low $50 deductible on your auto or homeowner policy is costing you money that could be working overtime for you.

By the wise use of deductibles, you can be working those extra dollars until you need the money. Your emergency fund is designed to support these minor losses.

Risk retention is certainly not a total solution. I have seen families who could least afford it take on insurance risks the average test pilot would not tackle.

Finally, you can *transfer* the loss through insurance. Though it is relatively easy to recover from a $250 deductible, you cannot recover quickly or easily from catastrophe —the loss of your home, a tragic medical disaster, a million dollar suit by a neighbor, or someone hit with your auto can cripple your goals for the rest of your life.

Never risk a lot for a little.

(If you think you can never have too much insurance or are always sticking up for your agent brother-in-law when the subject of insurance comes up at social occasions, you might as well skip this and the next three chapters. You have already been thoroughly brainwashed and would be better served to use these pages to train your next puppy.)

Insurance companies have their own principles for insuring the public. Simply stated, the less frequent the loss or peril and the more catastrophic it may be, the cheaper per unit the premium for coverage. Examine your auto policy and check the liability coverage you have. Compare that amount with the actual reimbursement if your car is damaged. You will find that a lot more liability can be bought for less money than it would take to replace or repair your car. In your homeowner policy, liability also costs significantly less than property damage coverage.

## The Winning Strategy

If you attempted to be insured against every loss, you would be "insurance poor." How do you decide which perils to buy protection for, and which dangers to self-insure yourself against?

Insure yourself first against those losses from which you could not recover—death, catastrophic medical costs, total disability, and liability. You can really recover from a fire in your home, even the total loss of your home. It would not be easy, but since you were still healthy and working, it could be done. How could you ever recover from a $500,000 or $1,000,000 personal injury suit against you and your family's assets and future earnings?

Next you should insure yourself against those losses which would cause you to borrow heavily against your future and other financial goals. This is where the damage protection on your dwelling and your car come in.

Heavy losses in these areas would adversely affect your financial goals over the short-term.

The areas you should *not* protect through insurance are the small but pesky losses—a $250 ding on your auto is not catastrophic (unless it is a Lamborghini), and if there is not enough in your emergency fund for the repair bills, you can usually find someone who loves you enough to bankroll you...this time.

## Everybody Sues Somebody Sometime

Clients frequently ask how much insurance is enough. My response is usually to ask them what kind of accident they are planning to have. I can only tell them statistically what amounts most claims are settled for. If you are a professional, plan on being sued for more. The "deep pockets" theory comes into play here.

Our society is definitely lawsuit-happy. What is the monetary worth of an arm, a leg, or an eye? Whatever a lawyer in a courtroom can convince a jury it is worth. Juries are swayed by a victim wheeled into a courtroom or a small child who has lost his sight. Juries also think they are giving away someone else's money and striking a blow for the underdog, the little guy. They won't remember that you are *also* a little guy, so little that you only have maybe $100,000 liability insurance. Foolish you.

Most of you probably believe that the primary purpose of your homeowner and auto insurance is to protect your home and cars from damage. If you have ever been sued, you know better.

Parents sometimes advise young adults that, since they have few assets, they need little liability protection. That is dangerous and short-sighted advice. A jury may award a large settlement based on the future earnings of a defendant. A young medical, law, or business student looks like an attractive future bankroll. The more assets you have now or *will have in the future,* the more likely someone will want to move in with you and share your goodies.

Parents also tend to think that once a child has reached the age of majority (from 18 to 21, depending on the state) their own assets can no longer be touched. If your child is still in any way dependent on you, you may be held at least partially responsible. Adults with college students and young adults starting out on their own with financial assistance from their parents are vulnerable.

I don't agree with this "sue, sue, sue" philosophy, but I recognize it is here to stay and that it is a serious threat to everyone. People change when faced with large medical bills or when bad things happen to those they love. Sometimes they convince themselves that enough money will somehow soothe the problem or provide enough punishment for the offender—you, the other victim.

The greatest benefit a homeowner or auto policy carries is *liability protection against the other guy.*

## Only 500 Indians? No Problem.

Most people buy insurance with the same foolhardy confidence Custer showed when he told the cook before setting out for Little Big Horn: "We'll be back before lunch."

You wouldn't buy a typewriter with half the keys or a set of "pre-punctured" tires. But many people pay exorbitant premiums for protection they don't need while *not* protecting themselves at all from far more critical (and more likely) occurrences.

And the companies certainly aren't trying to make it any easier. Insurance companies are well staffed with two categories of personnel: agents and lawyers. Both are paid by and owe their loyalty to the company that hands out their weekly paycheck.

You cannot rely only on what agents *tell* you you are buying. The wording in your contract *is what you have bought*, not the promises smilingly made over your kitchen table.

Some agents may misrepresent their products in an effort to peddle them. Others simply don't know enough about the coverage they're selling. In either case, you must know enough to be able to ferret out critical protection and exclusion clauses.

Unfortunately, pitting the average American against an insurance contract is akin to expecting Bambi to win the Kentucky Derby.

## Learning To Speak Insuranese

You will be unfit for battle until you understand what connection, if any, the legal jargon in an insurance contract bears to the English language. The following examples should make the *lack* of any connection clear:

*Accidental death:* Obviously, death that occurs from an accident.

*What It Means To Your Insurance Company:* Death must occur within a specified time of an accidental bodily injury independent of all other causes or contingencies including sickness, infection, surgery or other infirmities.

Philosophical question: If you were run over by a car and rushed to a hospital where you die two days later from heart failure, kidney failure, and excessive bleeding, have you died an accidental death?

Answer: Good question!

*Guaranteed renewable:* You can keep your coverage forever, even if you later contract severe health problems.

*What It Means To Your Insurance Company:* We can raise your insurance class rates to the ceiling to convince you to drop your policy.

**Waiver of premium:** If you are disabled and can't work, your premiums will be paid...forever, if necessary.

*What It Means To Your Insurance Company:* You are disabled and your premiums will be waived, depending, of course, on the exact *definition* of disability in your policy, which will be one of the following depending on the quality of the policy and the length of time you're disabled:

a)  You are disabled if unable to perform *one or more* duties of your *primary* occupation;

b)  You are disabled if unable to perform *all* of the duties of your *regular* occupation;

c)  You are disabled if unable to perform *all* duties of *any* occupation you are capable of by reason of education, training, or experience;

d)  You are disabled if unable to engage in *any* gainful employment (including, but not limited to, pushing a broom or stuffing envelopes).

**Accidental bodily injury by accidental means:** You accidentally fall off the ridge of your roof while attempting to fix the chimney on a Saturday morning. Your hospital bills will be paid by the insurance company.

*What It Means To Your Insurance Company:* You are covered only if the result of not sprouting wings before hitting the ground was *also* accidental; the cause or means of the accident must also be accidental.

It is not easy to convince an insurance company adjuster that you accidentally wandered up onto your roof and spontaneously began repairing it, perhaps under a sleepwalking spell, which is the only way to convince them that it *was* an accident.

I assume you're getting the drift here: *The bold print giveth and the fine print taketh away.* I have never seen the words "fair" or "friendly" in any contract, insurance or otherwise. *All* contracts are written by lawyers, lawyers who have *not* been paid by *you.* Pleading ignorance of what you have voluntarily agreed to in writing usually won't recover the losses you may suffer from buying an inferior product.

Always flip straight to the clauses marked "Exclusions and Limitations." That is where you will find more important information than anywhere else in the contract. An insurance contract that is ambiguous in a court of law will usually be decided against the drafter. Therefore, every word is important to the company. It should be to you also.

## Just The Facts, Ma'am

Getting the greatest value for your insurance dollar demands that you rid yourself of certain myths and fallacies.

**Fallacy:** Insurance companies' primary interest is your well-being, even at the risk of their own.

**Fact:** Insurance companies are profit-making corporations with stockholders who expect large bottom-line earnings. They are *not* charitable organizations dedicated to the consumer.

**Fallacy:** There *really is* a "free lunch."

**Fact:** Every day, by mail or telephone, you are taught you *can* get something for nothing. Though your intellect tells you this is not true, you nevertheless buy lottery tickets, answer ads to get rich quick, respond to sweepstakes offers, call about free vacations, and buy valuables supposedly well below normal prices.

Why not? Pictures of previous winners look *just like you,* common folks with goals and dreams that came true simply by returning a card or making one telephone call. Any references to such benefits from *any* salesperson should send shivers up your spine, not make your tongue hang out.

**Fallacy:** Today only—ten percent off! What a deal!

**Fact:** Ten percent off *what?* A product can be marked up significantly and then marked down...and still cost more than you would have originally paid! Oh, but you bought it on sale.

Only through an apples-to-apples comparison with similar products can you determine the real value of any purchase, including insurance protection. Look at the bottom line for the desired number and amount of benefits. Companies work overtime to create products which *can't* be easily compared to their competitors'. But just because it isn't easy doesn't mean it isn't important. When you suffer a loss, no one brings up how expensive your insurance coverage was. All anyone wants to know is how much coverage you *had.*

**Fallacy:** All companies are created equal and charge relatively similar premiums.

**Fact:** Even many insurance agents believe this, though it's completely bogus.

Your premium will depend on the following variables:

1) The loss experience of the company for the danger or peril covered;
2) The expenses of the company (which can be enormous); and
3) The investment experience of the corporation.

*Investment experience?* If a company has poor portfolio managers, *you* should not be expected to make sure it is still able to pay its stockholders their monthly dividend. But you will, because your premiums will go up accordingly.

In the same vein, the millions a company spends on advertising to attract new customers gives you absolutely no benefit at all...but where do you think they're getting those dollars from? That's right. They just increased your premiums *again!*

**Fallacy:** Only well-known companies are solvent and pay out claims.

**Fact:** Big is not necessarily better. It probably is not cheaper either. Does a TV ad really say anything important about a company's claims history, its value per consumer dollar, or even its real reputation? Insurance companies pay their ad agencies big bucks for ads that create a sense of stability, friendliness, good value, and even sexual attractiveness to induce you to buy.

None of that should matter to you. All *you* want to know is how much it will cost for the coverage you desire and whether the company will pay you if you sustain a loss.

I have heard agents remark that they refuse to compete on price. What *are* they competing on then? Their ability to fox trot, smile longer than another agent, read a rate card better? Some of the cheapest companies are also the most service-oriented and the most solvent. Because they don't advertise.

Don't be coerced into paying more for a "professional." If I needed a heart transplant, that term would mean everything to me. But shopping for insurance, I only want a solvent company with rock-bottom prices.

**Fallacy:** The larger the premium, the better the product.

**Fact:** In other words, the more you pay, the more you presumably get, right?

Wrong. Unfortunately, price is no protection from mediocre products, many of which are overpriced because of the higher commissions that must be built in to induce salespeople to market them to the public in the first place. The better the product, the *less* motivation a customer needs to purchase it (or a salesperson to sell it).

But be careful whose prices you compare. Calling the two or three largest companies in your area may net you nothing. Amazing! They all charge exactly the same for the same policies! Perhaps these companies aren't as unfriendly and competitive as you've been led to believe.

Each knows what the other charges for every product. Why start a price war? Aren't there enough customers to go around? P.T. Barnum has been proved right time after time.

For a true comparison, call those smaller companies rated high in consumer publications. You will find significant differences between companies and recapture savings for your other financial goals. Every company has its own set of losses, expenses, agent commissions, administrative costs, additional agent commissions, and expected profit ratios or earnings. You may even consider it your moral imperative to support less greedy companies whose products are of equal quality and more reasonably priced than the big guys'.

**Fallacy:** You should only work with one agent for all your insurance needs.

**Fact:** Do you only see one doctor for all your body parts, shop at one store for every item you buy, or always eat at one restaurant? Companies and their agents spend a lot of advertising dollars to foster customer loyalty, knowing that if the price on one product must remain competitive, they can always make up the difference on others.

If you don't mind paying more because your agent showers you with hand-holding, birthday cards, and occasional baby-kissing, you are cheating yourself. Your loyalty should be based on the answer to only one question: What have you saved for me lately?

**Fallacy:** "Updating" is just another word for improving your insurance program.

**Fact:** Every three to five years the industry develops another "new and improved" product (like soap powder), and unleashes it on the public via agents who will gain new commissions from companies which will earn new premiums.

Overselling and rolling-over policies is a popular pastime for some insurance agents. If you need new coverage *that* often, your insurance agent is not doing effective long-term planning with you. In some cases, you should probably be *decreasing* your insurance coverage as you and your property get older, *not* buying more and more.

## Winning The Insurance Game

Memorize the following game strategies before you purchase *any* type of insurance coverage:

1) All *policies* are not created equal.

2) *Some* policies are more equal than others.

3) There may be little or no relationship between premium cost and quality of coverage.

4) All *companies* are not created equal.

5) Insurance companies are in business to make a profit.

6) Company advertising creates name recognition —nothing else.

7) Company advertising costs *you,* the customer.

8) The bold print giveth and the fine print taketh away.

9) The agent does not share in a loss you sustain because of loopholes in the coverage he or she sold you.

10) Separate the written contract promises from the sales pitch.

11) There is no such thing as a "free lunch"— accepting such invitations will cost you dearly;

12) Every insurance company and its agents have a vested interest in your purchase of their products.

Special tip: When dealing with an agent with a large briefcase, hold out for a better deal. He or she *always* has something better and cheaper down at the bottom.

Finally, as your agent tools up in his or her fine new Mercedes, ask yourself, "Do I really want to deal with *successful* insurance agents?" Strange question? Think about it.

If they are successful, they are making a lot of money. Who is paying their high commissions? The insurance companies they work for. Where are *they* getting the money to pay those fat commissions? Guess who?

Personally, I would rather deal with some guy with a hole in his sock who was barely making it because he didn't make too much commission on each policy he sold.

Low-cost protection is still available. But don't expect an agent to voluntarily cut his own income when you are so willing to accept less. An agent who wants to make $100,000 a year can sell 1,000 policies and make a commission of $100 on each. He can sell 100 policies and make $1,000 apiece. Or he can sell just 25 policies and make $4,000 on each.

I can tell you from experience: It takes a whole lot of hustling to sell 1,000 policies in one year's time (or, for that matter, in an entire sales career). So how much do you think your agent is pocketing every time you sign on the dotted line?

In the next three chapters, we will look in more detail at the rules to follow and hazards to avoid when purchasing life (death), homeowner's, auto, health, disability, and long-term care (nursing home) insurance.

Study these chapters carefully—each can save you thousands of dollars.

## chapter six

# Life Or Death Insurance

---

You have built a beautiful new home, a dream for which you've worked long and hard. You expect the children to grow up in it, and you look forward to many pleasant memories. Your daughter will probably meet her first prom date in the downstairs hallway. Your small children will peek over the stairway bannister waiting for Santa.

The scary part is that this is probably the largest purchase you will ever make. And you know some disaster could occur. Lightning could strike. The home could be vandalized, damaged in a storm, even burned to the ground. You know it must be protected for your family. You don't like insurance premiums any more than your neighbor, because you're paying out good money but hoping you will never collect!

You invite your property insurance agent to your home, showing it off as proudly as if you were selling it. The agent does some thoughtful analyzing, some quick calculations, then makes a recommendation: "Your home will cost $150,000 to replace, but I would advise you to insure it for only $50,000 and start a retirement or college fund with the money you would have spent on the additional coverage. That way, if your house burns down, you will have $50,000 to start rebuilding. But if it *doesn't,* you will not have shelled out all those extra premium dollars for nothing, and you will have some savings for your retirement."

How long would that agent remain in your home? Would *you* be willing to underinsure your home by two thirds?

## A Time-Honored Argument

Despite that example, this chapter is *not* about your homeowner's insurance (see the next chapter). It is about your life (or, more accurately, *death)* insurance.

By now, most of you are probably aware of the perennial argument: Which is better—cash value life insurance or term death insurance?

Consumers have become increasingly aware that cash value insurance (marketed as whole life, ordinary life, limited pay life, single premium, single pay, universal life, and variable life, among other names) offers higher commission structures to agents and greater benefits to insurance companies than term insurance.

Therefore, many informed consumers have learned to decrease their insurance premiums by buying term coverage (which offers a death benefit only), even as most agents continue to tout the saving and investment virtues of the higher-priced cash value products.

My feeling is that we've been putting the cart ahead of the proverbial horse. Whether to purchase cash value or term insurance is the *third* question to ask. The *first* should be: *How much* death insurance do you need? The *second:* Can you afford it?

Whether cash value is the greatest idea since sliced bread or the worst financial rip-off in modern history is unimportant because *most families simply can't afford enough cash value insurance and* must *buy term.*

Most families don't look at their future earning power in the right light—as a paycheck *which will only continue if the breadwinner(s) remain alive and working.* Families whose fathers or mothers have died think of little else.

A home isn't the only dream you have promised your family—there are basic necessities such as food, clothing, shelter, utilities, and the retirement you and your spouse are looking forward to. All of these cost dollars, dollars which you expect to earn in the future. But if you are cut out of the picture, where will that kind of money come from?

If a young couple with a child or two (or more) has a $25,000 or $50,000 death insurance policy, reality is that if the breadwinner died tomorrow, the family would be broke within two or three years...at most. The mortgage would have to be paid off. The credit card companies would want their money. The car finance company would demand full payment. Doctor and hospital bills for your last illness would blossom. Not even the funeral director would wait around for his check ($5,500 in today's dollars).

Unless you leave behind the blueprints to Fort Knox, your family gets the pittance left over. And you thought you were leaving everything to *them.*

I have a major problem with insurance agents who underinsure young families with children and a home because their companies, which would rather sell a policy with a larger premium, motivates its agents to sell *smaller* policies with higher built-in commissions. Those agents and companies make a conscious decision to deliver a smaller check to the grieving family, a check that may only be a fraction of what they need to survive. It's a practice that should be illegal. It isn't.

I would rather see you insure your home for one-third of its value and buy enough death insurance in case you die. At least if your home burns down, you will *be* there to help rebuild it. But you can't come back and correct the mistake of buying too little death insurance.

# I'm Worth *That* Much?

So how much death insurance *do* you need? Agents seem to have ready answers. I am amazed that some of them can so easily pull a nice round number out of the air and, like the Wizard of Oz, make an instant recommendation for the amount of death benefit that will take care of your family. I am even more astonished at agents who leave the entire decision up to you, simply asking how much premium you want to pay.

Look at your homeowner and auto policies. Do you see any nice round numbers? No. The amounts you see are *exactly* what will be needed in case of loss. Death insurance works the same way. There is a *precise* amount that, if you died tomorrow, could be invested at a certain rate of return (after taxes) to pay off your debts, replace your present income, and keep your family going.

But arriving at that figure requires several pages of data, including a financial statement of your assets and liabilities, the ages of your children, the earning power of your spouse, whether you desire to fund some college for your children, your pension survivor benefits, and whether you want to fund your spouse's support after the children leave home.

A thorough insurance analysis should also include the value of any Social Security survivor and dependent benefits, the amount of term insurance you may have at work, and whether you want your family to be able to keep their home.

The result of all this analysis is that *most young families need between $250,000 and $500,000* of death insurance to provide sufficient payments when their children are young. How do those figures stack up against the amount *you* have been sold?

This is why the question of which kind of insurance is best—cash value or term—is a moot point for most of you.

There is simply no way an average family can *afford* enough cash value insurance. That leaves term insurance as the only option.

## So Just What Is Term Insurance?

Term insurance isn't designed to make you rich or provide you with any retirement benefits. If you don't die, you get nothing back. Just like your homeowner and auto insurance—if you don't have a loss, you get nothing back.

When you purchase death insurance, are you protecting your liabilities or your assets? If you won the lottery, how much death insurance would you feel you needed? Probably none. You are protecting your liabilities because you don't *have* the assets yet. You are protecting yourself as a money-making machine for your family during those years when your weekly paycheck is vital to support them.

When your child is two years old, you need income to support him for at least sixteen more years. When he is twelve, he only needs support for six more years. If you intend to fund a college education, you need a certain amount of insurance only until the child graduates.

So as you grow older, your liabilities tend to *decrease*. In the meantime, you are supposed to do everything you were taught in this book to become mercenary and develop your own assets that will protect you in your old age. You simply can't live and die at the same time.

Term insurance is criticized because as you get older, it gets increasingly expensive, to the point where you can't afford the coverage. But as you get older, you should have *fewer* liabilities to protect. So you should be *decreasing* your death insurance to match those liabilities and socking everything else you can into your own pocketbook. As you decrease your amount of coverage, you will reduce the premiums payable, and it will remain affordable.

Term insurance isn't advertised by the insurance industry as a whole. Agents don't want to sell it to you. If *I* ask an agent why, his answer will be that he can't make a living on term commissions only. If *you* ask an agent, you will hear other reasons.

They may tell you that with term, if you don't die, you won't get anything back. You *do* want something back, don't you?

Term insurance won't protect you permanently. Do you want to give up your insurance at age 65 because you can't afford it anymore?

You can't borrow from term insurance and get a cheap loan when you need money.

Finally, you really don't have the discipline to pay yourself first, and this will be a simple method of accomplishing that objective.

Those negatives can often talk you out of opting for term insurance. Even though we've already talked about some of these negatives, let's examine each in a little more detail and see how well these arguments hold up.

## One For The Price Of Two

If you buy any type of insurance policy, you get the promised benefits when you have a loss. Life insurance works similarly. When you die, a term insurance policy pays you whatever death benefit you've purchased. But so does a cash value policy—A $50,000 policy pays $50,000 when you die, *no matter how much extra money you have accumulated in your savings.*

Who gets the rest of your savings?

You originally bought two things—an insurance policy in case you died and a savings plan if you lived. But it seems like you only got one—the death benefit.

You're right. Why? Because that's the way it works. If you live to be 99 and have $49,000 in the savings portion of your life insurance, you would *still* only get $50,000 if you died. The *insurance company* would get to keep the $49,000 that was once your savings.

Something seems wacky here. If I purchased a three-piece suit (coat, skirt and vest), I am paying something for each piece, even though the outfit is sold for one price. After the outfit is altered, I expect to receive all three pieces back. (Wouldn't you?) I would not react cordially if the sale clerk asked me which *part* of the outfit I wanted—skirt, coat or vest? I *paid* for all three, and I *want* all three.

When you buy two things, you had better get two things, or you are not using your money wisely. And although you are paying for two things in a cash value policy, you only get one. It is this "bundling" concept that is the basic problem of cash value insurance.

If you are never going to put away any extra money, and you don't die, perhaps you are better off with the small amount of savings you will have at retirement from a cash value policy. Because of the time value of money and inflation erosion on future savings, you may not be *too* much better off.

Personally, I don't need (or want to pay for) a large insurance company looking after my money and working it for 40 years or more for themselves before I get my hands on it. Insurance companies, as a whole, have assets in the trillions. What are your assets? Can you afford that kind of expensive money management?

## I Can't Afford To Die?

The argument that a retiree may have to give up his or her insurance coverage because term insurance gets too expensive is persuasive. At a time when money will be at a premium, how can you afford to pay more for insurance? In a cash value policy, the savings portion is designed to help cover your retirement needs.

But, as we discussed above, if you take away your savings, your insurance coverage disappears. Because when you withdraw your savings from your policy, either in one lump sum or in monthly installments for the rest of your life, you give up your death benefit.

*So you will have no insurance coverage after retirement whether you buy term or cash value.*

Of course, there is a solution to the above problem, one your agent will happily point out to you: You can *borrow* the money out of your policy. You don't even (supposedly) have to pay back an insurance loan. Or even the interest on it. But you *will:* The insurance company will just keep taking payments of interest out of your cash savings until it is all gone. You know what happens then—your insurance self-destructs.

There are many astute people who have bought this benefit idea. It would take a bank a lot of creative marketing to convince people to put money into a savings account and then, when they wanted it back, encourage them to borrow their own money and pay interest on it.

Cash value is cheaper than term when you reach a certain age. Why? Because you pay more in the beginning (when you are young) so you can pay less when you are older. So how does the company make out? When you pay your premium into a cash value policy, the company immediately purchases a term insurance policy on your life, then invests the rest of the money.

*If term insurance is good enough for* them *to buy for* you, *why isn't it good enough for* you *to purchase for* yourself?

If you are depending on a savings or investment insurance policy for retirement, do you get a rebate for all those early years you overpaid? No. Does the insurance company get a giant profit for all those years it worked your money? You bet. That's how they can afford to pay out all those hefty agent commissions over the years. And still have a fat profit left over.

If death insurance is designed to cover your liabilities and replace your income, what are you doing with *any* insurance after retirement? Where is the income you are supposed to be replacing? Where are the liabilities you had when you were younger? At retirement your problem is not dying any more; it is living and finding enough cash to keep yourself alive in an inflationary environment of increasing medical costs.

## We're Just Here To Help You Save

The one argument that holds up in favor of cash value is that if the company doesn't force you to save, you probably won't save anything. With Americans saving 3% annually, they have a real point. If you are planning to purchase term insurance and fritter away the rest of your money, you should underinsure your family, purchase the higher priced insurance, and hope you don't die.

On the other hand, if you would rather work your own money and at age 65 have $50,000 in cash instead of a $50,000 life insurance policy, term is the solution.

## Good And Bad Terms

Before considering converting your insurance to term coverage, you need additional information about the three basic kinds of term insurance: (1) annual renewal or yearly term; (2) level term; and (3) decreasing term (also known as credit life).

*Annual renewable term insurance* has a level death benefit, but the annual premium for that amount of coverage increases each and every year. You are charged for one year's mortality at a time.

This type of term may not be able to be decreased over time, and its cost *will* eventually outpace a family budget, especially when you hit 40. It is, therefore, most appropriate when coverage is needed for a short time, such as two or three years. If you are contemplating taking out a large short-term loan for a business or other purpose, for example, this type of coverage is the most cost-effective way to protect your family from the extra debt in case of your death.

***Level term insurance*** has a level benefit *and* a level premium for a stated period of time. It can be purchased in increments of five, ten, fifteen or even twenty years without an increase in premium. Some term policies can be renewed automatically until the age of 90.

If you have a young family, buy a policy with the longest time period before any premium increase. If your children are older and your future need for death insurance is rapidly decreasing, the shorter time periods may be your best buy.

***Decreasing term*** (also commonly known as *credit life* or *mortgage insurance*) is heavily promoted to new home owners. *This is the most costly form of term insurance and the poorest buy.*

The death benefit in this type of policy decreases as your mortgage does... but the premium stays the same. So the most cost effective time to die if you own this type of insurance is near the beginning of the insurance policy. Near the end of the term, you are paying the same rates as in the beginning, but you are getting very little coverage for your money.

Be careful: I have occasionally found the mortgage insurance premium wrapped into the monthly mortgage payment, which means you're paying interest on your insurance premium. *This is illegal.* To be sure you're not getting shafted, contact your bank —ask them to isolate each charge that is built into your monthly mortgage payment.

There is a more serious drawback to decreasing term: The *lender is the beneficiary of your mortgage insurance policy.* Your family will never see one penny of that death benefit. If anything should happen to you, the institution will keep the death benefit, even if there are not enough other assets to keep your family fed and clothed.

What a clever marketing device! The lenders have discovered a method to cover *their* risk in case of *your* death through an insurance policy on *your* life with *you* paying the monthly premiums out of *your* pocket, with *them* as the beneficiary.

You probably *would* like to have your home paid off after your premature demise, but shouldn't your spouse have the *option* of making that decision if there are greater expenses or needs than the amount of death benefit you originally provided?

If this kind of risk management is attractive to you, please drop me a line. I would be happy to assist you in purchasing—and let you pay the premiums on—a $50,000 life insurance policy with myself as the beneficiary.

Lenders may demand that you have mortgage insurance sufficient to cover the amount of the mortgage loan, but they cannot demand you buy it from *them.* When you buy a new home, add a rider (an additional amount of insurance coverage) to your existing term policy. Gracefully decline your lender's gracious invitation to further profit from you.

## The Winning Death Insurance Strategy

Purchase a policy whose benefit can be reduced at any time, and re-examine your financial position every three to five years. As your mortgage decreases, your assets increase, and your children get closer and closer to going out on their own, reduce the face amount (death benefit) accordingly. Then use that reduction in premium to increase your assets even more—every time you reduce your death benefit, add the premium difference to your present investments. You will be gradually transferring money spent on *dying too soon* to the impending problem of *living too long*.

Eventually, you should need *little or no* death insurance.

Insurance companies base premiums on data from large random samples. Seek the lowest risk group for your specific situation. If you are a non-smoker, consider only a non-smoker (not standard) death insurance policy and a company that penalizes smokers by charging them much more. If you are a good driver, find those companies who are hard on substandard risks or very restrictive in their enrollment. If you have no teenage drivers, there are companies who will be cheaper because they decline so many young people. If you are accident-free, don't hook up with a company that will insure almost anyone.

On the other hand, if you are a poor risk, choose companies that tend to lump together good and bad risks. That way another policyowner is paying part of your real premium. Group insurance is a good example. Rates are based on the average age, occupation, and health of the group. Individuals may pay the same premium, but separately offer various risks to the insurance company. If your health is poor and you can get into a relatively healthy group, your cost will be absorbed by the other members of the group.

Finally, before you buy any life insurance (or any other insurance, for that matter), request that the agent trying to sell you sign the following declaration:

## An Insurance Agent's Personal Contract with A Client

The advice I have given you during the time we have spent together has been totally objective and in no way based on any self-interest or any monetary benefits I may gain as a result of your purchase of my products. I have thoroughly explained all available options which could accomplish your objectives, regardless of the difference in commissions I may receive on various products.

All advantages and disadvantages of any product have been presented. I have also provided a full disclosure of any and all hidden costs or internal charges involved in each product. My recommendations are based on the most cost-effective method of accomplishing your financial goals.

All information presented is the result of expertise in each area I have presented myself to be a professional. All recommended solutions are based on your unique financial, personal and risk tolerance objectives. I offer you the relative assurance that these solutions will withstand the test of time.

I have acted first and foremost in your best interest and in a manner consistent with the highest standards of honesty, integrity, and ethics.


_____
Agent


If an agent is truly ethical, he or she will sign that statement. If you later find out that you were not advised of material facts which would have caused you to *not* purchase the product, then hold him or her to the written word... in a court of law, if necessary.

If an agent balks at putting his or her name on the verbal promises he or she has made, show him or her the door.

| chapter seven |
| --- |

# The Good, The Bad, The Unnecessary

I hope you never have an experience like Art.

On vacation with his wife and two children, he received an emergency call from his mother—his father had suffered a stroke. The family quickly packed and flew home, accidentally leaving one suitcase, Art's expensive camera, and the children's water skis in the hotel lobby. The airline lost the other suitcase.

Art's wallet, still chockful of credit cards and money, was stolen by a pickpocket in the airline terminal.

When he arrived home, he found the front door ajar, the house ransacked, and the color TV, his gun collection, his wife's jewelry, his son's coin collection, and the remainder of his camera equipment gone.

During the burglary, Art's St. Bernard dog had evidently escaped from the house, gone next door to spend some time with Yvette, the neighbor's show dog in heat, and pillaged a vegetable and flower garden during a playful chase. The dog had also romped with the neighbor's toddler, leaving several scratches, which the neighbor felt were worth quite a penny in pain and suffering.

The upstairs balcony glass door was wide open, the apparent escape path for the thieves. Unfortunately, it had rained, and the bedroom carpet, valuable furniture and bedclothes were stained from sitting in the water for the past week. Electrical cords leading to security light timers had been shorted out. The chain reaction had blown a fuse in the main service entrance, setting off a surge of power to other appliances, including the refrigerator and the full freezer of beef and other previously-frozen food. Water lying on the soaked upstairs bedroom floor had leaked through and stained the downstairs living room ceiling.

After Art collected himself, he called his insurance agent to report the disaster. The next morning, the agent examined the losses, quietly listened to Art's unbelievable story, then told him the bad news.

The homeowner policy Art owned was just a broad form, so it did not cover indirect damage to appliances, spoiled perishables, or flood and water damage "other than by breakage of glass or direct damage by lightening." Art had no special Scheduled Property riders to cover the full value of the jewelry, the camera equipment, or the coin and gun collections.

Art had not added an inflation guard endorsement to keep the home insured for at least 80% of its replacement value through the years. Therefore, none of the losses would be totally covered anyway. And since an owner has a responsibility to protect damaged property after a loss to prevent further destruction and limit an insurance company's losses, there was a question of coverage for any of the downstairs water damage.

Art had actual cash value instead of replacement coverage on his personal contents, so he would receive only the *depreciated* value of any stolen or damaged items, not what it would cost to replace them—much more. The theft of Art's wallet was not reported to the police. So there was a question whether that loss would be verifiable and, consequently, covered.

The dog's actions, to some extent, *were* covered, but since Art's liability was lower than his agent had originally recommended, the maximum amount available for legal defense and liability damages would be limited to the pittance in Art's policy. Which would pay for a lawyer with holes in his socks...maybe.

Finally, the agent advised Art that if the thieves had suffered any injuries during their theft, *they might sue!* And, believe it or not, *they might win,* even though they got injured while committing a criminal act.

Most people wouldn't wish this much bad luck on their worst enemy. This story might even be laughable, except that the losses Art sustained are commonly restricted or even excluded in some homeowners' contracts.

Remember the story of the three little pigs? Keeping the wolf from your door is the major reason consumers purchase insurance. I have seen some horror stories and some sad endings. I can also count on my fingers the clients who really understood what they had purchased.

People never get beyond the insurance legalese. Most let their agents make all their decisions for them. Some never open their policies to see if they even have the kind and amount of protection they thought they'd bought.

## Homeowner Insurance

This type of insurance is relatively easy to understand and compare. Find your latest declaration page (which is not the real contract but only a summary of amounts) and examine it for the following:

1) The limit of liability coverage;
2) The basic form of the policy;
3) The amount of coverage on the dwelling and other structures;
4) Replacement or depreciation (fair market value) coverage on the dwelling;
5) Inflation guard endorsement;

6) Personal property coverage—including the overall limit, whether coverage is for replacement or actual cash value, and your Scheduled Property list;

7) Total premium per year; and

8) The loss deductible.

## Liability

Liability protects you if you are sued or held responsible for another party's loss or injuries. $100,000 is *not* enough coverage. Many agents are now recommending a base policy of $500,000 and an umbrella policy of up to $1,000,000 extra coverage. Attorney fees and medical bills can add up quickly.

You have an even greater liability risk if you own any of the following:

1) A teenager;

2) A pool;

3) A pond or recreational lake;

4) An old shed or unused dilapidated barn;

5) Vacant land;

6) Swings or other playground equipment that attract neighborhood children;

7) Any item in disrepair—an old fence, an unfilled well or cistern, an open ditch, or an old tree that could lose limbs during a storm;

8) A pet—dog, cat, or horse (dogs no longer are entitled to one free bite before owner responsibility sets in ). "Beware of..." and "No Trespassing" signs are of very limited protection;

9) Accessible electrical wires or any unusual and unprotected electrical outlets or appliances.

This list is far from comprehensive. Go through your home and yard, looking for conditions which should be repaired, filled in, or otherwise made safer.

If you own bare land or unoccupied dwellings, they are potentially more dangerous because they can attract children and teenagers. You may not care if the buildings are replaced, but sufficient liability protection is a must. One match or one cigarette in an old barn can trap a child in a raging inferno. You may have to give one company all your business to motivate them to cover this situation.

Even a trespasser may have a claim if you can be proved negligent. Small children are considered incompetent to assess the presence of danger and have been awarded large settlements *even if they trespassed or climbed fences to gain access to property.*

Liability is limited to individual and noncommercial pursuits, not business or rental ventures. Don't expect your regular homeowner's policy to cover you for a home occupation, special business, or rental property. If you own storage facilities which you rent out or real estate investment property, you need additional coverage.

The insurance company must defend you (unless the loss was intentional or an act of war) up to the limits of your liability coverage. Some companies will settle quickly to save money from a drawn-out court litigation (though they may later sue the other party or the party's insurance company to collect any damages they paid you).

No one wants a claim history on their record which then may increase their insurance premium for up to three years. So there is a temptation not to report relatively small mishaps or collisions when you feel damages can be ironed out on an informal basis. Be careful. Always report losses as soon as possible, whether or not you plan to collect from your company. Otherwise, if you are later sued or a loss claim is filed, your company need *not* defend you.

A frightful number of verbal parking lot agreements end up in litigation. Stories change. The responsible party

later claims no responsibility. Perhaps someone had mor
extensive injuries or damage than immediately suspecte
Tracking down someone who is attempting to avoid yo
later is difficult. Proving the supposed offender was eve
at the scene of the damage or injury without witnesses c
a police report may be impossible.

In a court of law, it is often one person's word agains
another's, and a judge's interpretation of whom he think
is telling the truth may decide a case. Get police documer
tation and notify your insurance company so they can b
prepared to defend and protect you if necessary. Savin
future premiums in this manner is not wise. A perso
with two prior accidents or damage claims may promis
anything at the scene. Later, self-interest and surviva
instincts take over.

Umbrella liability policies have become popular due t
recent astronomical court and jury settlements. An um
brella policy fits tightly above both your homeowner an
auto policies and can be added for a relatively sma
annual premium, adding $1,000,000 or more to your basi
liability protection. Its deductible is whatever liabilit
coverage you have on your basic policy.

Monetary crises bring out the best and worst in peopl
Your friend could as easily turn into an adversary as
perfect stranger. That neighbor's child you baby-sit fo
who stays at your home after school until her parent
come home from work, or the children who like to play i
your yard because your toys are so much better tha
theirs, are all candidates.

When I hear a couple remark that their friends woul
never sue them or want to extract money from them,
become frustrated. They are not watching or reading th
news—or they would know that this situation happens al
the time. People can justify many things when they fee
they have nowhere else to turn.

An umbrella policy is a small price to pay for reas
surance that you will not have to raise someone else'
family or provide years of future income for a stranger.

## Your Basic Coverage Form

Homeowner policies come in several basic types: HO-1, HO-2, HO-3, and HO-5 for homeowners; HO-4 for apartment dwellers and other renters; HO-6 for condo owners. Most folks are oblivious to what form they have.

HO-1 and HO-2 are only broad forms of coverage and are *not* enough for the average homeowner—I refer to these as "call if it burns down to the ground" policies because they leave out many common perils. Most homeowners need greater covered losses and fewer exclusions. Unless you are a slum landlord, you probably need better quality coverage

HO-3 provides all-risk coverage on your dwelling, better coverage on contents, and transfers more risks to the insurance company. For most homeowners, an HO-3 does a reasonable job of protection.

HO-5 is the cream of the crop. You may want to explore this option if you have an unusually expensive or custom-built home. Compare the increased benefits to the substantially higher premiums.

## Dwelling Coverage

The dwelling figure will need to be maintained at either 80% of the total cost of replacement (minus land and foundation) or 100%, depending on company policy. Most claims, such as kitchen fires, furnace or chimney fires, water damage, or theft, are not total losses. An astute consumer might calculate that, since the risk of losing his entire home in minimal, why not reduce the coverage and insure it for only 50% of its replacement value to take care of the more common accidents that might occur?

The insurance company is ahead of you. If this strategy were to catch on, perhaps everyone would want to insure only a portion of their home's actual value. This is

where the 80% rule comes in. Unless that dwelling figur
stays above 80% of the current cost of total replacemen
the company will refuse to pay 100% of *any* loss, partial o
otherwise.

How can you tell if the present figure is sufficien
Divide the dwelling amount by 0.8. This will tell you if yo
are above the coverage demanded. For example, if you
dwelling figure is $80,000, $80,000 ÷ 0.8 = $100,000. Ca
your home be reproduced for that amount? If you fee
uncomfortable with the present figure, contact your agen
and invite him over for another appraisal.

The disadvantage of using only the 80% figure as you
limit is that the insurance company's maximum paymer
to you will be only $80,000, even if the house burns to th
ground. If you actually feel that it will cost $100,000 to re
place your home (at present construction costs, *not* marke
value), and assuming you *want* it replaced, insure it fo
$100,000, not $80,000.

## Replacement Or Fair Market Value

Replacement coverage generally puts your home bac
together as closely as possible to its condition before th
loss. It is not designed to make you a profit. Actual cas
value reflects only the fair market value, which will b
potentially much less, and probably will be different. Yo
do not want fair market value unless there is such a larg
differential between the premiums for replacement an
costs for market value coverage that replacement is no
affordable. Some century-old homes cannot be insured fo
replacement value due to their present market value ve
sus the astronomical cost of redoing them in the gran
manner of the past. Receiving a check for $40,000 for th
total loss of an older home will buy only part of the new on
built on the same site.

Many folks think they have replacement coverage o
their home when, in fact, they have depreciated or fai

market value. Either find it in your contract or call your agent and get a written record on his letterhead to that effect.

## Inflation Guard Endorsement

Inflation endorsement coverage is an optional rider that makes good sense. It allows the dwelling coverage (and premium) to creep up yearly to match increased construction costs in your area. It will usually be quite small, less than 5% per year. But it is vital to keep your home adequately insured.

If it is not automatically done through a rider, the temptation is too great to forget to increase your premium every few years. (Who likes to call an agent and request that *more* money be taken out of one's pocket?) You will be risking a lot for a little if you have not kept up with inflationary costs of construction.

## Personal Property Coverage

Personal property coverage ranges between 50% and 100% of the amount on your dwelling, depending on the company. Check for replacement coverage. If the ten-year old TV set is stolen, a check for depreciated value from the insurance company for $25 will not go far. A five-year old couch will likely bring only a few dollars from an insurance adjuster.

If you do not see replacement coverage on your declarations page, contact your agent and get it in writing. It is important to understand in advance what you are not covered for so that any gaps can be corrected.

In our original story about Art, some of his losses centered around several expensive items of personal property. No insurance company will take additional risks on unique or special items without a corresponding increase in premium. Your contract will spell out the limitations on such categories as jewelry, money, securities, collections, statuary, and fine arts.

If you wish to increase these limits, you must add a Scheduled Property endorsement, which will list each item and its appraised value. Discuss with your agent what constitutes Scheduled Property. Have these items individually appraised by a reputable company at today's replacement values, send the appraisal to your company, and keep a copy for your records.

Otherwise, you will suffer a monetary as well as an emotional loss if they should disappear. Collections take years to accumulate. Don't compound a personal loss with the added problem of being underinsured.

Photographs should also be taken when possible and stored elsewhere. Be sure each special item is listed on the policy when you receive it, and have it reappraised every few years. A company will only pay up to the maximum amount you have stated. Inflation can outdate appraised values in no time.

If you own collections, list numbers, editions, or serial numbers along with your appraisal. An artistic piece you value highly may look like an *au*tistic piece to an insurance adjuster lacking receipts or other supporting documents. Attempt to keep receipts for large items. The adjuster works for and is paid by the insurance company, not you. He may attempt to be fair and equitable, but he will *not* be overgenerous and help you make a profit.

In my home, we have a holiday tradition. When the family members come together, each is given paper and pencil and told not to return until at least one room is inventoried—all contents. This includes underwear, dresses, lamps, pictures, and numerous other items that may seem of little consequence. After a loss it is virtually impossible to remember everything that may have existed. A current inventory also adds credibility when you want to collect.

An even better idea is to produce your own video on a room-by-room basis. Film all walls, floors, and even ceiling fixtures, and zoom in on any special items. Store this somewhere other than your home.

Important deeds, security certificates, wills, and insurance papers should be copied and stored in a safety deposit box or in a fireproof box away from "hot spots" in your home. They may also be kept near an exit to grab if there is time during a fire or other disaster.

## Your Premium

When comparing total costs, get an apples-to-apples comparison from each company so you can compare premiums for the same coverage. Build your own policy. For each category, compare the premium versus the benefits promised. Check several options for liability limits. For a few more dollars per year, you can usually get a lot more coverage.

Ignore any gimmicks such as safety discounts or sales that may be true for that company but not reflect true comparative value with another company. You don't care how many savings features there are. What is the bottom line?

## Deductibles

Loss deductibles may well be misused premium dollars. Any agent who will sell you a $50 deductible but leave you vulnerable in liability coverage is not working in your best interest. How many times have you collected on your deductible over the last five years? That extra premium has been working for someone else over the time. It should be working for you.

By raising deductibles to $250 or even $500, you can reduce your premium and keep that extra money working in your interest. When you have a loss, dip into your emergency fund for the amount of the deductible. You can often improve the overall quality of your policy by repositioning it to create high coverage in other areas and raising your deductibles. It is more important, over the long-term, to be adequately insured in catastrophic areas.

Don't pick a really high deductible if you have very little in your slush fund or emergency account. Get several quotes for various deductibles to choose which level is best for you. You can recover from a $250 loss, but most of us are friendless when looking for a $50,000 loan. You cannot repair this after an accident or a loss. You will simply become another sad statistic. Insure yourself properly against the most dangerous risks.

## Auto Insurance

By now, the following checklist of auto insurance do's and don'ts should give you a sense of *deja vu:*

(1) Buy the highest liability you can afford;

(2) Raise those deductibles;

(3) Compare the big company prices with those from smaller companies' and independent agents'—their rate may be cheaper;

(4) Check claim satisfaction ratings;

(5) Consider dropping comprehensive and collision when the car is six years old (unless it is a Rolls);

(6) Talk to others about their claims experiences with any company you consider; and

(7) Add an umbrella policy above your ordinary liability limits (especially if you have teenage drivers or other special risks).

Place both homeowner and auto policies with the same agent if possible. This buys a little extra insurance if you become more accident prone with your car, especially with an independent agent. An agent may consider retaining your auto coverage if he is afraid dropping you will cost him your homeowner business. But don't do this no matter what the cost. The agent must have low prices on *each* product in order to get your business on *both*.

The risk management principles here are the same, with one exception: If you have a teenage driver in the family. Teenagers spend most of their waking hours networking with each other to improve manipulating their parents, Yet parents, who should be more clever, spend little or no time working out defensive patterns for teenage attacks.

Kids stick together. Parents attempt to survive the teenage years with as few therapy sessions as possible, asking vague questions like why nothing worked on *their* parents like their kids make it work on *them*.

My son, who shall remain nameless due to my fear that, as a law student, he is probably at this very moment learning how to sue his parents, was the prototype for the entire series of Rambo movies, though we didn't get any of the royalties. His answer to all problems was simple—if a barrier was in his path and it didn't move on warning, he barreled it aside.

But that was just a warm-up for the day he turned sixteen and announced that driver's education was starting the following day. I knew it would not be long before he would start manipulating me to drive the family car. But I was ready—I did not intend to cave in like so many other parents I had seen. Would he be any different than the other sixteen-year olds in the neighborhood who leaped over small buildings with a single acceleration? I didn't think so.

I knew that "trust" would be a big part of his offense. Telling him he could only be trusted to drive up and down the driveway until he was married would set him back emotionally in other areas I had struggled to encourage and nurture. How do you tell your child you don't trust him? If you are smart, you don't.

A Mother's Answer: You tell him you don't trust the *rest* of the world. An accident won't be *his* fault. It will be the fault of all the *other* people in the world who can't be trusted. He won't end up in someone else's living room still buckled in the driver's seat by his own hand. Some stupid developer will have put that house right at the turn in the road that won't support an orbiting missile at 60 miles an hour.

I was simply not about to give him a weapon which could so easily kill him or another human being (especially when driven by a teenager intent on reaching speeds above Mach One). Not this mother. At least not until I found him a responsible wife. Then he could become *her* problem, and she could stay up and worry.

His father, though, saw only the positive side of this emerging opportunity. So he disagreed with my eminently reasonable parental position. My son cleverly used the "what's the use of having a temporary if no one will ever let me drive" scenario on his gullible Old Man, who caved in immediately.

The two of them will take to their graves what really happened, but their first drive together lasted 72 seconds ...and they never made it out of the driveway. Granted, the car was a standard shift and he had only practiced on an automatic. And, of course, the railroad ties lining the edge of the driveway were only eight inches high and could not be expected to hold back a 2,000 pound vehicle.

I knew I could eventually restake the ten-foot saplings —all three of them—that somehow loomed in his path and blocked his view of the rest of the yard he was digging up. I held back tears when I saw the row of blueberries I had raised from seedlings mowed down in the prime of their young lives. I would replant.

But I could never understand how both of them remained catatonic long enough to make it all the way to the neighbor's bean field. There was little said for more than a week. A mother's intuition strikes again.

Eventually, we all mutually negotiated a program of earned rewards: When my son showed enough general maturity to handle life's smaller challenges, he could get his permanent driver's license. That strategy failed miserably because I refused to admit that staying mature for 24 hours before he reverted back to his normal Godzilla approach to life fulfilled his part of the bargain.

The remainder of his teenage years were spent in relatively normal pursuits, except that female dates picked him up, drove him around all night, and dropped him off at home.

Though my son carried temporaries too numerous to count before he ultimately earned the right to a real driver's license, I will always feel this sole act of "tough love" may have saved his life, the lives of others, our assets and our home, not to mention our total sanity every time he would have left the sanctity of our driveway.

To those parents with invincible teenagers who want to hang in there a little longer, as I did, I have some final advice: Ignore the verbal attacks, the voodoo dolls in the kitchen cupboards, and the guilt heaped on you because everyone else's parents trust them and, therefore, you have as much sensitivity as cabbage and are totally heartless.

You are not *really* the meanest parent who ever lived.

That distinction belongs to *me*.

## chapter eight

# If You Can't Push A Broom, You're Covered

Health insurance follows the same risk management principles already discussed. The main elements in any policy are:

(1) Maximum lifetime payment (how much *in your lifetime* the company will pay, *regardless* of how high your medical bills climb);

(2) Coinsurance provision (the percentage of the bill you pay);

(3) Stop-loss limit (the amount at which the company starts paying 100% of all eligible covered expenses; and

(4) The deductible.

Think in terms of catastrophic loss. Find the highest maximum lifetime benefit. Look for unlimited benefits. A tragedy could wipe out your family's savings. You may have little choice under an employer's plan, but opt for the highest benefits before considering deductibles.

Co-insurance percentages vary. The less you pay out of pocket, the greater the premium cost. If your employer is funding the plan, you may care little about premiums. If you have an individual policy, keep the premium down by choosing at least a 20% provision for your payment portion instead of transferring the total risk to the insurer.

A stop-loss limit is the total out-of-pocket limit you will pay within a certain period, usually a year, before the insurer will pay 100% of the additional expenses. That should be reasonable, depending on your emergency fund and short-term savings to back you up. The lower the stop-loss breakpoint, the higher the premiums.

The deductible should be $250 or even greater if you have other methods of covering small medical emergencies and expenses. Some two-income families have two employer plans that can be utilized. They can overlap in this area to fill in gaps in one spouse's plan.

Stay away from mail order or TV insurance offers, even if they come with your latest credit card. The insurance is high priced and probably contains very limited benefits you won't understand until you need it (which will be too late). Never buy through advertisements. Compare companies every three or four years. Losses change over time. So do premiums.

Don't buy insurance of any kind that comes with a "free lunch," such as a period of free coverage. Avoid any gimmicks or offers of discounted sales come-ons. A good product doesn't need to be marked down.

Fledgling countries have seceded from their motherlands more easily than you will get a bargain with policies that promise you cannot be turned down and require no physical of any kind. Older people are particularly vulnerable to sales pitches because they are terrified of becoming a burden to others or outliving all their savings. Their grown children can protect them by being present when any solicitations or presentations are made.

Any product sold to an unhealthy older person will probably be misrepresented or contain so little real protection that it is not worth even a small premium. It upsets me when the elderly use their pension or Social Security dollars to pay for life or supplemental health policies that are not reputable. Their present problem is living, not dying, and keeping as much money as possible for their own needs.

If you are self-employed, request quotes for several deductibles and compare premiums versus benefits. If you have young children or an accident-prone family member, the lower deductible may be more attractive. Add up last year's medical bills and see which benefits you more.

When considering whether to add maternity, dental, or supplemental accident benefits, compare the additional premium for each benefit to the amount you perceive you will be able to benefit from in the future. For example, the cost of maternity benefits must be compared to the number of times you expect to use them.

Dental coverage may not cover preventative or annual visits, braces, or any cosmetic surgery deemed "medically unnecessary" by the insurance company. Supplemental accident riders (which pay the first dollars for emergency accidents) may be cost-effective if you have any accident-prone family members, such as children. Change your benefits as time and your family's personal and medical life change.

HMOs (*H*ealth *M*aintenance *O*rganizations) can be beneficial if you want first-dollar coverage and either your employer will fund coverage or you are willing to pay the additional premium dollars. One caution: HMOs usually have staff doctors that you must use. Your personal doctors may not be included. You may be more comfortable or feel more confident with your choice of medical professionals. You may also want a doctor who thoroughly knows your medical history and one whom you already trust. You must be released by the HMO before they will pay costs for outside medical care, and they may be reluctant to release you until they have exhausted their own diagnostic staff.

Workers often assume their employee medical benefits will fit every situation and cover them for every contingency. Get that employee benefit book out and go through it carefully. Learning too late what you haven't got is like trying to put the genie back into the bottle. He just won't listen to you anymore.

## Disability Income Protection

Protecting future income is the most commonly overlooked risk. If you fell off your roof next weekend, who would continue to work for you and bring in the weekly paycheck? If you were seriously injured in an auto accident tonight, who would feed your family until you went back to work? If you never worked again, what would you do? I don't wish to sound heartless, but if you had sufficient life insurance, your family would likely be in better financial shape if you *died*.

Total disability is a greater financial disaster to your family than your death because there is no individual death insurance benefit at work. There will be increased medical bills and continued rehabilitation and therapy costs. There will be no more paychecks at a time when you have not built up a significant pot to live off. Your wife cannot remarry because you are still here, and there are often small children who will become more expensive as they grow older.

I hope I've convinced you of the importance of disability income protection. But let me also caution you about the care you must take in ferreting out the *right* coverage. Which I will do with yet another story:

A scorpion, a natural predator of the frog family, needed to cross a deep creek. She presented herself to a frog sunning on the bank and offered to pay the frog handsomely to carry her across the creek on its back. The frog justifiably refused this dangerous proposition, reminding the scorpion that it was basic to her character to kill frogs.

The scorpion rationally explained to the frog that it was in her own best interest to allow the frog to live and even to prosper because the scorpion would also drown if she attacked the frog in the water. After some thought, the frog agreed to the expedition.

As the strange-looking twosome approached mid-stream, the scorpion violently stung the frog with her poisonous venom. The frog, realizing that he would soon be only history, was outraged. He screamed at the scorpion: "Knowing full well that you are about to drown, too, why have you done this tragic deed?" The scorpion, lowering her eyes, answered, "I am not evil, nor am I stupid. But above all, it is my basic nature to sting and kill frogs."

Disability companies and their products vary so in quality that some are worth less than the price they charge just to administer the contract. Disability insurance is also so confusing that it rarely takes up much space in insurance "how-to" books. Like the scorpion, as long as the free enterprise system prevails, it will be the basic nature of some companies to exercise their right to sell the lousiest product at the greatest profit.

Most workers assume their employment disability or Worker's Compensation will suffice. In fact, most Social Security claims are denied, and group employer plans can be very restrictive and offer little protection against long-term total disability.

At best, disability benefits replace only a portion of your prior income, usually no more than 60%. Look through your employee benefit booklet and compare it to the strategies in this chapter. If the list of limitations or exclusions is longer than that of jobs around the house you didn't get to yet, or if your employer doesn't even offer any long-term disability benefits, you need your own disability policy.

## Fluent In Insuranese Yet?

Disability policies can hide more traps than an 18-hole golf course. The specific wording is crucial to the quality of the contract because there are so many definitions of disability. When buying a product, request a specimen contract and compare it with others before choosing both the company and the particular policy.

Disability coverage has two parts: (1) short-term (up to three or six months) and (2) long-term (from six months on). Companies tend to offer better short-term disability packages because they are less costly to the employer. But it is vital to have a secure long-term disability program— you can limp over a three- or six-month period without income; no one can handle the loss of all future income.

The crucial elements of long-term disability coverage are:

1) The definition of total disability;
2) Noncancellable and guaranteed renewable clauses and a guaranteed rate;
3) Length of benefits and maximum monthly benefit;
4) Elimination period; and
5) Social Security disability benefit integration.

To remind you of our earlier discussion, there are a variety of ways the company can define "disability":

1) Your inability to perform *one or more* of your *primary* duties of your *present* occupation;
2) Your inability to perform *all* of the duties of your *regular* occupation;
3) Your inability to perform *all* of the duties of *any* occupation for which you are suited by reason of training, education or experience;
4) Your inability to perform *any gainful employment*; (including broom-pushing, envelope-stuffing, and dog-walking).

There is a world of difference between each of the above definitions. Those differences in contract terms will determine whether or not you will actually qualify for benefits.

*Your* definition and the insurance company's may be totally different. If so, just remember who generally wins and loses such arguments.

## There's Always Another Agent

If you are a firewalker or a weekend crop duster pilot, you may be limited in the kind of disability coverage you can find. But if you have a less-hazardous occupation, you should opt for the most liberal definition of disability you can buy. If you are told by an agent that you cannot qualify for a better plan than the one he's offered, check with other companies before settling for less. Companies have different standards—you may be able to qualify for a better contract with someone else.

The contract should state that it is noncancellable *and* guaranteed renewable at a guaranteed premium. This means that the company cannot cancel your contract in the future unless you change to a more hazardous occupation *and* cannot raise your premium. If your policy is "guaranteed renewable" *or* "noncancellable," it means the company has the right to raise your premiums as a class as high as their little profiteering hearts may choose.

Renewable or optionally renewable speaks for itself. You have a gun with no bullets. All the options for policy renewal or premium increases are at the discretion of the insurance company. All future bets are off.

The length of time for benefits is next in importance. Lifetime benefits for accident and sickness are optimum, followed by benefits at least to age 65. Benefits for five years or less will be of little help when you are facing a total disability for the next 30 or 40.

An inflation clause or option to purchase additional income benefits is an obvious advantage because cost-of-living increases will be necessary as inflation outpaces your monthly fixed income check.

The elimination time may be chosen by you and will determine when, after a loss, you want to begin collecting the monthly income checks. Use the same strategy that works for homeowner and auto coverage. A longer elimination period (90 to 180 days) will decrease your premium significantly. Lengthen the elimination period for a larger monthly benefit or longer benefit period. Income from vacation pay, sick pay, Worker's Compensation, severance pay, short-term disability employment benefits, or your IRA funds can cover the gap until your policy disability benefits kick in.

You can add a Social Security integration rider, which, if you qualify for disability under the terms and conditions of Social Security (good luck!), will reduce your regular disability income check by exactly the amount the government provides you. If you do not qualify for Social Security (60% or more of original claims are disallowed), you will lose nothing because the insurance company pays you the originally promised amount. By agreeing to seek Social Security if you are disabled, you may decrease your policy premium further.

If your employer pays your disability premium, your benefits are taxable to you. If you pay your own premiums, the income is tax-free.

Worker's Compensation may be integrated and expected to cover occupational injuries. Your private insurance may be only a secondary carrier. Watch for these limitations. Changing to a more hazardous occupation without notifying your insurance company may void contracts due to the increased risk the company must bear, a risk of which it is unaware.

There are many disability insurers in the field but few that will be around with a quality product far into the future. Spend fifteen minutes at your library researching company solvency and policy options. Consumer publications spell those out.

Don't let a discount expert sell you a policy. Collecting on it may be Slim to None...with Slim on vacation in the

Dominican Republic when you need him. The best policy for you will NOT be the cheapest. Shop for the best value at the best price.

## Long-Term Care Or Nursing Home Insurance

These policies often have so many limitations, the fine print spelling them out takes up more space than the big print telling you what they cover. And they can be so misleading that it's difficult to give you all the ammunition you really need to protect yourselves from the many inferior products out there.

But here goes anyway. Consider this the mini-course you need before you listen to *any* sales presentation for long-term care or nursing home insurance. It will highlight and differentiate the few quality products from the hundreds of others flooding the market.

If the policy requires prior hospitalization before entering a nursing facility, pass it up. Quality companies do not have that limitation. Policies should not restrict certain conditions or diagnosed diseases—such as Alzheimer's disease or certain types of cancer. A policy should protect you no matter *what* type of disease you contract.

How many days of nursing care are allowed? The best contracts currently allow up to four years of nursing home care and lengthy levels of step-down care.

In this market, a cheap policy may very well mean an inferior one. Research local nursing home facilities to discover their daily rates, and purchase enough daily coverage to protect you from future inflation. $70-$100 per day is an average daily benefit in most areas of the country today.

Consider foregoing a short elimination period (the length of time before the policy benefits kick in) in order to pay for a larger daily amount of coverage. Like any other product, increasing benefits in one area may subtract coverage from more critical area in another part of the contract. You will probably be better able to afford to pay *in full* for a nursing home for 30, 60 or even 90 days than to make up $20, $30, or $50 a *day* for years.

Is the policy noncancellable and guaranteed renewable? Just as in disability insurance, the words "guaranteed renewable" by themselves are not enough. Believe it or not, I have seen more than one contract that states it is "guaranteed noncancellable," but then outlines the conditions under which the company can choose to "nonrenew" the policy.

When filling out your application for coverage, be sure all medical questions are answered completely and honestly. Some companies use "misinformation from insured" as a favorite basis for disallowing future claims. Be sure you read the final medical application after the agent has completed it and before you sign it. Insist that the agent add any pertinent information, whether he or she thinks it "important" or not. Remember: The agent will always get his or her commission, even if you never receive any benefits.

Research the company issuing the policy you are considering in the library. No one can accurately assess the actual costs of medical care, and a company that finds a product is not profitable could simply decide to drop it. If you develop medical problems in the meantime, you may not be able to purchase coverage from another company.

Every word in the entire contract should be read and clearly understood before you add your John or Joan Hancock. Do not be lulled by "agent translations" and explanations. They may be comforting...and misleading. Remember the key lesson from all our discussion of insurance: You are purchasing exactly what is written in the contract, not what you are verbally promised.

Compare policies from several companies before making any decision. Request a specimen contract so you can read it over carefully and see exactly what you're buying.

If one is not available, scrutinize your policy as soon as it arrives. You will have a short period to return it and receive back your full premium if it is not what you want.

If you do decide to return the policy, be prepared to hold your ground against the agent's most urgent ministrations: He or she has already received a commission and may try virtually anything to change your mind.

Never respond to fear sales tactics or believe that a specific policy is the only contract available to you because of your current health. Do not be pressured into signing by an aggressive sales pitch. If it is a good policy, it will still be available tomorrow, next week, next month.

It is unlikely you will find a contract with all the benefits and provisions you desire because the risks associated with current health care costs are so uncertain. As America grays, costs should become easier to project, and nursing home contracts will, hopefully, be a more secure bulwark for the older consumer.

Until that day, examine these policies as if your life depended on it.

It probably does.

| chapter nine |
| --- |

# Your Biggest Investment...
# Certainly Not Your Best

There are few subjects that evoke as much emotion and patriotic defense as the concept of owning a home, the cornerstone of the American dream. Home ownership has come to symbolize an American birthright, and invariably represents the largest single purchase most of us will ever make.

If concepts presented earlier in this book have challenged your preconceived notions and time-worn, hand-me-down lessons, this chapter will contradict virtually *everything* you have been taught by your parents, the lending institutions, the real estate industry, even the United States Government.

To set the stage for the controversial ideas which follow, let me tell you another story:

There once lived a mythical fox whose fur was full and luxurious, especially his fine russet tail. He was secretly admired by all of the other wildlife, especially for his tale.

Over time, the fox became vain and self-impressed.

One day, while preening himself along a riverbank, he lost his footing and slipped down the bank, barely missing a large muskrat trap set by a hunter. Only his tail was caught. He sighed, greatly relieved that he had not been mortally wounded.

But as nightfall approached, the weather grew cold and the fox, still shackled by his trapped tail, began to worry about how to get out of the trap. Try as he might, he could not get his tail out of its gripping claws. Later still, the river grew colder, ice formed on its surface, and the fox's beautiful tail was frozen beyond repair.

The fox examined his options, lamenting that to save his life, he would have to lose his beautiful tail. A sad but determined survivor of nature, he broke off the frozen tail and fled back to his forest home.

When the other forest creatures saw his injury, they were at first bewildered. Since the fox had said nothing, they whispered among each other until a rabbit finally confronted the fox. Embittered by his own loss and self-interest, he spoke up defensively.

"Nonsense!" exclaimed the fox. "This new look is my own invention and a clever one, too. It will be cooler in the summer, cleaner and lighter to carry around with me, and let me run faster. Mark my words—it will soon be the fashion in the forests around us."

As the animals circled the fox, little by little they began to appreciate the improvements the fox had made. Eventually, all the creatures of the forest cut off their tails so they, too, could profit in the obvious ways the fox had.

The moral of this story: Whether you are purchasing a home, a melon at your grocery store, or a used car, what you pay will depend on what the market will bear and the quality of the sales pitch, *not* on what the product or item is worth in real benefits to you.

## The Myths You Probably Believe

Say goodbye to the notion that houses always beat inflation, that they are risk-free investments, and that they should be the first investment on your list. That propaganda has begun to unravel because it has already seriously hurt many people who were counting on their home appreciation to pay for retirement and other critical financial goals.

Whether you should own a home or rent an attractive appliance carton for the next 20 years is not the issue. My argument is that you should simply not believe the bunk you have been fed by the foxes of the world—buying your personal residence is *not* the wisest investment you will ever make.

## Anyone For A "Pig In A Poke?"

When is the best time to buy a new home? Just ask a real estate agent, broker, or lending institution: RIGHT NOW. This very minute. Don't even wait until after breakfast. If interest rates are low, buy before they go *up*. If rates are soaring, buy now before they go *higher*. Can't afford a reasonable down payment? Don't worry. That's what creative financing and government money are *for*.

Don't know how long you will stay in an area? Buy that house now and when you move you can take your profits or rent it out and have a monthly income. Can't afford the monthly payments? No problem. Just spread them out over 30 years, giving you *lower* payments that can *easily* be squeezed into that already sagging monthly budget.

Thinking about renting for a while first? Good heavens, you don't get anything *back* when you rent. Look at all the equity you could be building up in a home instead of making a landlord rich.

## Meet The Foxes

The real estate industry makes its money by moving real estate and ONLY by selling real estate. When money comes in one door, it must go quickly out another. What can the average American do with loaned money? Why, he can buy real estate. So the lender finds its market by perpetuating the virtues of home ownership.

The federal government must find ways of keeping the country expanding and citizens employed. One bellwether of the nation's general economic health is housing and housing starts. So Uncle Sam also has a vested interest in encouraging you to purchase the American dream.

The building industry turns its product over to the real estate industry which feeds the banking industry which turns to the government for guaranteed backing (which the government gets from us).

This flawless circle is unbreakable *as long as all those in the circle propagate the same information*. Even if lending institutions get stung by bad loans or mismanagement —have you been reading the headlines about the S&Ls and growing danger of Third World debt?—they will be bailed out by the government, who will simply come back to *us* to get the money to do so. This keeps the economy flowing.

The government even discriminates in favor of the building, real estate and banking industries through little games it plays with the taxpayer, offering tidbits all too many of us grab as fast as a lake full of ducks heads for the guy with the bread.

Homeowners can have home interest tax deductions, tax-deferred profits, VA and FHA programs, GNMA and FNMA guarantees, investor securities in various packaged home mortgages, federal home loan programs, bond issues, first homebuyer incentives, rehabilitation project subsidies, Senior Citizen housing project investor programs, additional tax deductions for home equity loans, and a plump one-time $125,000 profit exclusion after age fifty-five...

And this is only *part* of the iceberg.

Can you think of *any* reason why even *one* of the above groups would advise you *not* to buy your Dream House? None that would benefit *them*.

## Here's My Heretical View

All these merchants offer a giant menu: With a home you can have status, an inflation hedge, tax write-offs, a sound, low-risk investment, increased value through improvements, the pride of ownership, marketability, greater privacy, and a proper environment to raise a family.

After all, this is the American Dream.

But compare real estate to a bank CD as an alternative investment. Can you sell your home as fast as you can cash in a CD? Does a personal home throw off monthly or quarterly income? Can you purchase a unit as small as that of a CD? Since your portfolio should always be diversified, is it unbalanced due to the large amount of money you have wrapped up in a home? Since most advisors recommend that not more than one-third of your total portfolio be in real estate of any kind, if you own a $50,000 home, do you have another $100,000 in other investments?

What about liquidity? Are you sure that every dollar you put into a home you can get out at sale time? The costs of buying and selling plus improvements and maintenance over time must be subtracted from your eventual profits. If you rent, these expenses are the responsibility of the owner, and you are free to move when you want. The most you can lose is your security deposit.

The costs of borrowed money over the life of the mortgage are not even whispered in the presence of a potential buyer. Do you know how much you will eventually pay for that $60,000 home? On a conventional 20-year mortgage, you will fork over *twice* the amount you thought you borrowed. Over 30 years, you will hand out over *three times* the original debt. A home would have to double in price every 20 years just to keep even *on that point alone*. On a 30-year loan, you would have to get three times the price you paid. The average home is not appreciating at anywhere near that pace.

What about this sound and low-risk investment concept? Does real estate always go up? Try to convince homeowners in Houston or Louisiana, where people simply boarded up their homes and walked away from their mortgages when employment dried up. In the early 1980s, banks in Ohio and Michigan had more homes than they could resell. In the Northeast, some homes will lose 10% of their value...this year.

Even if a home appreciates over time, have you considered the costs of insurance, real estate taxes, assessments, improvements, maintenance and buying and selling costs?

Inflation, the deadly money killer over time, is another factor that cannot be ignored, since it increases housing prices more than any other element. Even though inflation seems to be performing wonders on your real estate, it is also increasing your costs in every other area. If inflation increases your home's market value 6% a year along with other prices, you have made no real gains. If inflation moves even higher and your home does not keep pace, you are actually losing ground—your home is really *depreciating* over time, due solely to the decreasing value of money.

## You Won't Believe These Numbers

Before you become totally convinced that I am anti-American and don't support private home ownership for individuals, let me explain. If you can afford a Rolls Royce, by all means buy one. If you can spring for a yacht or a mink coat, then reward yourself and your loved ones. If you can afford a home, you should have one to raise your family.

But to buy the most expensive home you can squeeze into your budget with the conviction that you are pursuing a sophisticated and effective investment strategy is sheer folly.

I have suggested that when you to add 2 + 2 the answer should always equal 4. Forget for a moment the defensive posture you may have built up as you read the first few pages of this chapter. Use your common sense and apply the lessons from earlier chapters, plus a little math.

Let's assume we know an older couple who purchased a home 20 years ago for $25,000 and have just sold it for $75,000. Ignore for the moment the costs of the mortgage, improvements, maintenance, taxes, insurance, closing costs, points, and real estate commissions. Also ignore the opportunity costs—what else their money could have been doing for them during that 20-year period. The home never needed painting, nothing ever broke, and the bank pitied them and gave them the mortgage money free.

How much did they make? The simple answer is 200% over 20 years, and that is what you are encouraged to believe.

But it took 20 years to make the 200%. By applying a little simple math, that means they actually earned 5.647% per year on their initial $25,000 investment. Isn't that great? Instead of getting the 8% to 9% per year they could have earned from a variety of investments—with no extra fees, no hassle, no maintenance, total freedom from buying and selling, liquidity, instant marketability, and a government guarantee of principal—our couple opted to invest at 5.647%...before taxes.

Wait a minute. That's a lot better return than it should be. Why? Because we specifically exempted all other costs associated with owning a home from those calculations. So let's ask our couple to rejoin the real world and look at what their home really cost them over that 20-year period.

First of all, our couple didn't have $25,000 to invest. They made a 10% down payment—$2,500—and borrowed the rest—$22,500—on a 20-year mortgage on which they were charged 10% interest.

When they bought the house, they had to pay a 7% real estate commission ($1,750) and $2,000 for closing costs and points on their mortgage. The mortgage they signed called for monthly payments of $215.34...for 20 years—$51,680.

While they owned the house, they had to pay property taxes ($600/year), insurance ($200/year) and keep the house in reasonable shape ($500/year). This all cost them $26,000 more over those 20 years.

Finally, when they sold the house, they had to pay a 7% real estate commission on the proceeds (7% of $75,000 = $5,250). There were probably some additional closing costs, though we have been kind and left them out of our calculations.

So including the down payment, insurance, property taxes, minimal maintenance, closing costs and real estate commissions, and the cost of the mortgage money, this couple paid out a total of $89,180 over 20 years. And they walked with the $75,000 they sold the house for.

**Conclusion: They paid out $14,180 more than they sold the house for!**

Wait a minute, you gag. That can't be right. Real estate is a great investment. You must have done something wrong. Aha, you left out tax deductions!

First of all, we were, as I said, kind. We left inflation completely out of the picture, figuring that insurance cost the same when the house was worth $25,000 as when it was worth $75,000, for example. Ditto with property taxes. And we only included minimal maintenance. Over 20 years, one would have to add *some*thing for major repairs, additions, exterior painting, repairing major structural damage, or landscaping and improvements which are not saleable but which improve living quality and comfort. Adding *any* additional outflow of money, including the inflation on insurance, property taxes, etc., and this calculation looks even more horrible!

Ah, but what about taxes? Well, we'll look at the tax question in a little more detail later in this chapter, but for the sake of the argument we haven't finished yet, we'll be kind again. Let's say that every penny paid out—all

$89,180—was fully deductible. And, even better for our hypothetical couple, they made a lot of money (despite their inexpensive home) and were in the 50% tax bracket for all 20 years. (We'll ignore the Reagan tax cut for the moment, giving our couple far more than they deserve.)

The result would be tax savings of one half the total spent, or 1/2 x $89,180 = $44,590. Therefore, if our couple sold the house for $75,000, but only spent $44,590 after taking tax savings into account, they made a net profit of $30,410.

There, you chortle. That's more like it!

## Feeling Better? Just Wait!

Not so fast. First of all, please admit that I have now given our couple every benefit of the doubt, *underestimating* expenses, *ignoring* inflation, giving *hefty* tax breaks the IRS would blanch at. Agree? And the result was a profit of $30,410, right?

Now, let's be *really* heretical. Our couple decided they just couldn't afford that house. Instead, they rented for the entire 20 years and invested the money they would have put into a house in a variety of vehicles on which they earned 8% a year, a modest return (especially during the inflationary '70s!). We need to make one assumption here before we compare how they would have done this way— that they could have rented a nice place for $215.34/month —exactly equal to their mortgage payment—not an outrageous assumption if houses were selling for $25,000!

Then what did they do? First of all, instead of turning over a $2,500 down payment and $3,750 in closing costs, commissions and points at the very beginning, they took this $6,250 and invested it for 20 years, reinvesting all the interest earned along the way.

Once a year (at the beginning of the year) for 20 years they took the $1,300 they would have spent on taxes, insurance, and maintenance and invested that as well.

And, at the very end of the 20-year period, they had the $5,250 they would have had to pay for real estate commissions sitting in their checking account, not even earning any interest (yet!).

*The result, using annual compounding* (not even monthly) *is that they would have $98,631 at the end of 20 years—more than three times as much as they made from owning a house.* And that's presuming that they actually made a profit from our overly generous tax savings. If they had, as we originally calculated, lost nearly $15,000 by owning, the difference in their pockets is over $113,000.

Oh, there was maintenance on the house they rented—but the landlord paid it. And we probably should consider some small amount for contents insurance (though not building), and their rent would go up from inflation. And, of course, none of this money—that huge $215.34 in rent every month—is deductible. And they'd have to pay taxes on their earnings. *But at least they have income to pay taxes on!!!*

This really is an accurate comparison, if somewhat simplified. And it leaves out two very important points:

1) Only in some major metropolitan areas like Boston, New York and Los Angeles would our couple's home have ever *tripled* in value during that period. For most of the country, doubling would have been a more realistic assumption.

2) In virtually any case, no matter what the economy is doing and whether it is a buyer's or seller's market, you can generally rent *at least* (or more) home or apartment than you can buy. In other words, if you can afford a monthly mortgage or rent of $1,000 a month, you will generally be able to rent a nicer home or apartment than that money would buy you.

Despite these numbers, I am not telling you to rent forever or live in the streets. I merely want you to understand the absurdity of attempting to pass off the Great American

Dream as the wisest investment one can make. Sadly, most people never do the above math and don't discover how they have been duped. They continue to buy again and again, each time a bigger home with an accompanying bigger mortgage, right up to the day they retire. Then they wonder where all their money went!

## There's A Lesson Here!

There is one clear lesson from all this: If you *do* decide to buy a house, buy the one you need, not the largest and grandest one you can afford. *And invest the rest of your money somewhere else.* Your home may be the biggest investment you ever make. It may be the lousiest investment you can find. But it generally won't hit the top ten as the *best* investment you ever made.

Of course, there are exceptions to every rule, even the Rule of 72. We probably all know friends and neighbors who bought a home at a distress sale or purchased in hot areas of the country and "made a fortune" (their words).. But nothing lasts forever. Values peak and then decline. You may have even bought in at the bottom. But you probably won't get out at the top because you won't want to sell at the peak (greed clouds a great deal of common sense). The home generally plods along under inflationary pressure, while it saps up money which could have been put to better use.

You only have so many dollars in your lifetime to make work for you. Mortgage payments are made with seed dollars, right out of your paycheck. They never have a chance to work for *you*. If you purchase a $60,000 house and pay the lender a total of $120,000 for it, you have already spent $120,000 of the total you will earn in your lifetime. Since the median yearly take-home pay for today's adult worker is $20,000, you only have, on average, $800,000 over your working lifetime to use for all financial goals. And you've already spent 15% of it on your house.

Other housing costs outlined earlier will sap up many more of those original dollars.

This is one more reason the older generation has not been able to accumulate more for retirement. Their largest investment was generally their home. They didn't even average $20,000 per year during their working years, and they didn't count on inflation.

You have been taught not to analyze costs and to ignore the time value of money and the ravages of inflation. You have heard this fiction so many times that you may now believe it must be true. After all, everyone says...

## But I'm Cheating The Taxman!

Even if you are now convinced that your home loses something in translation as an investment vehicle, at least you may feel you have a viable tax shelter, just like the rich, to thwart the taxman. Before I congratulate you for practically stealing money with the tacit approval of the IRS, let's examine your home as a tax shelter.

By definition, a tax shelter is an investment which becomes more attractive because of some type of tax advantage—deferring or eliminating taxes makes the investment return more favorable. We've already seen in our first example that assuming some tax deductibility made the difference between a $14,000 loss and a $30,000 profit. But we were a tad over-generous. Let's look at another example, using 1990 tax rates, to see what what tax advantages really do to the value of owning a home.

Assume you buy a home for $62,500, using a 20% down payment of $12,500. You borrow the remaining $50,000 at an 11% fixed interest rate for 20 years. Your payments on this mortgage will be approximately $516/month for 20 years. We'll also assume, for the moment, that you are in the 15% marginal tax bracket—the lowest out there. Here is how those mortgage payments are applied (for the sake

of simplicity, I have just looked at the first and last years
of the mortgage):

| Year | APR | Payments | Interest | Principal |
|------|-----|----------|----------|-----------|
| 1 | 88.2% | $516 x 12 = $6,192 | 5,463.90 | $729.30 |
| 20 | 5.7 % | 516 x 12 = $6,192 | 352.74 | $5,840.00 |

The first year, $5,463.90 goes toward interest and $729
toward principal (or home equity). So you have a whopping
$5,463.90 in qualified residential interest to deduct off
Schedule A of your 1040 tax form. A 15% tax bracket
means that each dollar in deductions is worth 15¢ (15% of
$1.00) in actual tax savings. That means you have saved
$819.59 in income taxes (15% x $5,463.90). Sounds great,
right? You sure showed old Uncle Sam.

But you *paid* $5,463.90 in interest to get that $819.59 in
tax relief. There is an extra $4,644.32 still left. That is
money you paid out of your pocket and did not get anything
back for. For some reason, people think this part disappears. It doesn't, but it *is* "money out the window" unless
the appreciation of the home makes up for it.

In a 28% tax bracket, the interest paid gives you
$1,529,89 in actual tax savings, but $3,934.01 of *that* interest payment remains. Yes, you get to deduct *all* the interest, but you only get 28% of tax savings; the other 72% of
interest is "lost." Even though you have been taught that
residential interest is 100% deductible, that concept is misleading. You only get to deduct part of the interest—a 15%
or 28% tax write-off. It sure sounded better the other way.

If you have done your own taxes lately, you will notice
that Schedule A has been dieting and is getting skinnier
each year. The only significant benefits remaining are
residential real estate interest and real estate property
taxes.

Did you take the Schedule A total this year or just the
$5,200 standard deduction (if you are married)? Without
any itemized deductions at all you could have received a
$5,200 deduction. If you managed to squeeze out more than

$5,200 in itemized deductions, then you took the larger number. But instead you had to give up the $5,200 giveaway that anyone, even a renter, could have had...without spending a dime.

How valuable was your home interest when it cost you $5,200 to get the total on Schedule A? Unless you own a mammoth mortgage or had enormous debt levels or catastrophic medical expenses, you probably just took the standard deduction, after turning somersaults for a few hours trying to come up with more than $5,200 in deductions. If you itemized, you lost the standard $5,200 deduction, so your home interest *cost* you that $5,200. If you gave up and finally took the $5,200 standard deduction, you lost ALL of the value of your home interest—the whole 100%, not just the 85% or 72% from the tax calculations.

Those of you who are up to your eyebrows in monthly mortgage payments that rival the national debt—have you really won? That high mortgage debt is going to cost you dearly over time. An $800 per month mortgage payment over 20 years amounts to $192,000 of your take-home dollars. Can you really afford that much on one financial goal when you have college, living expenses, and retirement still to come?

Over the years more and more of each payment is applied to principal and less and less goes toward interest. Therefore, you have less and less each year to use as an itemized deduction. However, as that 20 years unfolds, you are probably getting *more* successful and making *more* money. You may have moved up to the 28% or even 33% marginal tax bracket. *But you have less interest to claim than when you were in a lower tax bracket.*

If a tax shelter was attractive to you when you were in the 15% or 28% tax bracket, it should be even more vital when you move up the tax ladder. Instead, you are moving in the opposite direction. You created a dilly of a tax loss when you were in a lower tax bracket. Now that you *need* maximum tax relief, you have less and less interest to deduct! In other words, you created a tax shelter when you needed it *least*. You didn't cheat Uncle Sam after all; you have literally *helped* the IRS, bless your heart.

## I'll Just Churn That Old House

Now you may think you are ahead of me on this count, figuring you can beat the game by buying and selling homes more frequently, every ten, or even every five years or so. That way you are always deeply in debt, purchasing a more expensive house each time to defer your taxable gain (profit) from the previous sale.

If you ever looked at a loan spread sheet and saw the actual percentage of money that went toward principal during the first few years, you would be in danger of total paralysis. As we saw earlier, the actual percentage of interest to principal in the first year of a 20-year loan is 88.2%! You thought you got your loan for 10% or 11%. A loan shark might give you a better deal in the first few years of a mortgage.

Do you understand why the lender gave you the original mortgage money? It wasn't a favor, after all. He knew that most folks don't default on their mortgages in the first few years, and the institution's risk of default would be pretty well covered if you defaulted later. He simply believed you were good for at least a few years. With that kind of leverage, and lenders paying you only 5% or 5.5% on passbook savings accounts as a lure to deposit the very money you may be borrowing for your mortgage, no wonder bankers work in large buildings with impressive staffs and furnishings and always seem to be smiling!

## Pay That Sucker Off In Seven Years!

Ah, you've found a way to beat me again—just prepay the mortgage. Pay it off in 10 or 15 years instead of 20 or 30. That will sure save a pretty penny!

True...up to a point. At the end of the loan, the percentage of interest to principal is much lower than at the beginning, as low as 4% or 5%. Many people are prepaying their mortgages near the end of their mortgage period to get it over with, since they may now have a little extra money each month to throw at that obligation. But that old ethic of paying your bills immediately *will* cost you.

At this time in your life, what is the next impending disaster—I mean, financial goal? College or your retirement, neither of which is probably very far off. Remember the lesson about compound interest and time—the less time one has, the more money (seed dollars) must be invested to achieve the same goal. By prepaying your mortgage, you are forking over extra money each month to the lending institution—which is certainly not grumbling because *they* don't want a 5% loan on the books either. They will be very cooperative if you give them the extra money you will need at retirement to amortize your loan faster and allow them to loan out this extra money they hadn't counted on to new, anxious couples.

Instead of stashing that extra money away in your own investment sock, you are giving it away for someone else to work. You will have a comfy feeling—your mortgage will be paid off earlier than expected. But you will also need a comfy feeling in your stomach from three meals per day after retirement, which you are going to endanger with this strategy.

Prepaying a mortgage is a positive idea from one point of view. It can reduce a mortgage down quite a few years. But it can also eliminate any early money you can put away over a period long enough to let *time* do most of the work. Remember the story of our twins, Bob and Bill? Remember how little money the first twin invested to make nearly $500,000 dollars? Only $12,000. Because he had so much *time* to work his money, he could use the rest of his seed dollars for other goals.

If you give your early money to the bank and end up with a paid-off home but a retirement or college stil.

needing funding, you will have lost so much of the time that you will have to contribute much more in seed dollars to achieve your goal. Would you rather spend $12,000 from age 22 to age 28 to make half a million or $60,000 from age 35 to age 65 to get the same money? Prepay the home by age 45 and *then* start on your half-million dollar goal, and you will need $7,936 each year (at 10% per year) in total seed dollars to accumulate your pot by age 65.

You thought you had managed to steal good information from the rich and here you are victimized again. Why do you think everyone was so anxious to accommodate you? When the self-interest of the financial industries agrees with your strategy, chances are you had better rethink your position. Early money always works better and faster. The later you put away that money for each goal, the more you need to save or the higher the rate of return (the greater the risk) you must utilize.

The glory days of the 1970s are gone, and so is the surging demand which kept inflating the prices of housing. Instead, you must now implement game strategies to protect *all* your total future goals when you buy, improve, or sell a home.

The Greater Fool theory states that even though you purchased an overpriced commodity, there is a greater fool out there somewhere who will buy it from you at a profit.

You may not always be able to fine a fool greater than the one whose shoes *you* wore.

| chapter ten |
| --- |

# Buying Your Money Pit Anyway

According to the latest survey, the median house in the United States can be purchased for a mere $93,000. When you recover from that statistic, you will either 1) assume that an even greater fool will eventually buy your home from you at an even more outrageous price or 2) realize that real estate "costs" whatever the consumer will pay, and the American public is being seduced.

Checkbook clutched in hand, the average homebuyer sets out to negotiate the largest purchase of his or her life with as many effective tools and defenses as David carried on his way to meet Goliath...minus the slingshot.

## Bewitched, Bothered & Bewildered

Purchasing a home is a highly charged and emotional experience milked for all it's worth by each group that will benefit from it. The average couple approaches this journey without suspicion and in a backwards manner.

They search for a home with an agent, whose commission is paid by the *seller*. They qualify with a lending institution which is *begging* to loan out money...for a profit. And usually fall in love with the most expensive home they are shown (which benefits both of the above), *then* feverishly attempt to figure out how to pay for it.

Perhaps the wife can learn to cook dandelions and wild mushrooms so they can save on food costs. The husband may offer to take lunch to work for the next twenty years. Promises made in the heat of passion for a new home are not admissible in any court of law. The $50, $100 or $200 extra payment tacked on top of a mortgage you can barely afford anyway is rationalized away at the time but rears its head later in the lack of monthly savings after the home is bought.

A smart seller will host an open house that bears a striking resemblance to a major revivalist tent show, with fresh flowers in every room, no sign of children and their respective messes (they are usually sent to the neighbors' to demolish *their* home for a few hours), and brownies baking in the oven. No human can resist this much temptation. And the agent is not exactly hoping that you *do* resist.

Remember when you bought your last car and were finalizing the costs? "Oh, you wanted *interior* seats? That will be only a little extra. How about tires to keep the car off the ground? No problem. Just let me add that. You know, someone in your position should have the velour upholstery, not that tacky vinyl. No problem. Just a titch more."

You know the feeling—you are being reeled in like a fish and don't know how to break the line. If you're ready to purchase a home and sign your life away on the bottom line for the next 20 or even 30 years, you need an approach to insulate you from these common sales tactics.

## Doing It Right

The appropriate place to start purchasing a home is at your kitchen table, with the family budget in hand. Look at the budget formula I proposed—you were advised to keep your mortgage payments under 22% of your monthly take-home pay. If you're ready to do so, you're ready to proceed.

## "Why Do You Want So *Little?*"

Visit your favorite lending institution, preferably with a 20% down payment in hand, and pre-qualify for a loan on a 15- or 20-year mortgage only *(not* on a 30-year life sentence) with affordable monthly payments, using your budget as a guide. The lender will probably assure you that due to your splendid credit record and secure employment, you could have a *much* bigger pile of money to take home with you. Just *ask* him.

At this point you must clear your head and figure out who your real friends are. In addition to your new home, you also need an emergency fund, a college fund, and the money to fund a comfortable retirement. Your lender, on the other hand, *wants you to buy the biggest house you can qualify for.* He or she is *not* thinking very much about your emergency fund, college for your kids, or your retirement.

If you stick to your budgetary guns, this may not be a fun session for your lender. You may notice a series of twitches cross his or her face when he or she can't talk you into a bigger pot of gold. Don't let that bother you. The lender will recover within the hour—as soon as a more willing (and pliable) buyer walks through the door.

What kind of loan is best for you? What about a fixed versus an adjustable mortgage?

Two major points should be explored. If your lending institution attempts to make you feel like pond scum for asking about points, rate caps, maximum rates, and what those rates will be based on, you are in the wrong institution. These terms (and their explanations!) can be so confusing that you *must* make sure you fully understand all your options. Have the loan officer run several options on paper for your examination. You will probably want to talk to more than one lender.

Adjustable rates have an attractive low initial rate but can increase substantially if you remain in your home for many years. In general, the longer you intend to live in your new home, the more important a fixed payment may become. If you are planning to live in a home for only a few years, purchasing it in the first place may be suspect —there will be too little time to develop any equity and recover your initial purchasing costs before trying to resell it, pay the reselling costs, and, of course, attempting to reap some kind of profit on the sale. If you are considering an adjustable rate, have the lender run a projection of the highest possible payment under the terms you are considering. If this looks outrageous according to your budget, take a closer look at a fixed rate loan.

Adjustable rates tend to favor lenders. No financial institution wants to be locked-in to low rates when interest rates shoot up. Adjustable rates allow a lender to maintain its profit spread no matter how high interest rates move. If rates climb 5% in five years, your mortgage payment increases quickly enough to keep the lender's profit margin intact. If interest rates fall, there is a tendency for mortgage rates to decrease more *slowly*. The lender benefits, you lose. Both ways.

Do not automatically feel that any institution that asks you to sit down is doing you the favor of your life. Lenders loan money only when they can make a profit on you. You should remain in control. Lenders should compete for *your* business. Take your time. Each dollar you spend in this area will take one dollar away from another goal, so guard your pocket jealously.

## How To Sound Like A Broken Record

When you are fully qualified for the loan, it's time to go house hunting.

As you prepare to confront the first real estate agent, practice your "broken record" strategy. You may not be familiar with this tactic, but you should be—it's the technique your children have successfully used on you since they were toddlers. No matter what the sales agent says or does, your response must always be the same: "I have only $\_\_ per month to spend for a mortgage, insurance, and taxes and only $\_\_\_\_\_ for a down payment, so I can't afford a house that costs more than $_____."

If the salesperson has seen this tactic before and immediately starts discussing last week's football scores in an effort to unsettle you, don't change the record. Eventually, though perhaps not willingly, the salesperson will give up and begin showing you houses you can actually afford. But don't let down your guard too quickly or easily —there are some very seasoned and determined salespersons out there.

Just keep remembering how much it cost you the last time your *kids* won. That should bolster your resistance.

## Finding Undervalued Property

Since you are attempting to make this purchase look as much as possible like an investment, there are several rules for finding undervalued property. First, look at the general neighborhood around a home you have spotted. Neighborhoods improve and appreciate, hit their peak, then depreciate. How can you tell which kind of neighborhood you are visiting?

One good clue is the number of children you see and the kinds of toys they are playing with. If a group of neighborhood youngsters playing by the curb looks a lot like the weekly meeting of the local Hell's Angels chapter, you should immediately return to the car and search elsewhere. (Don't walk, run, with purse clutched to chest.)

Your potential neighbors can fill you in about the neighborhood in general and your potential new home in particular. A neighbor may remember the family rowing out in front of the home after the last big storm. People may not be vocal about things they are pleased with, but they will be more than happy to share their misery with you—and every other rotten piece of local dirt and gossip.

You should contact county or city planning agencies to inquire about existing or proposed roads and other facilities. The day after you move in is *not* the best time to find out you have bought the house next to the proposed toxic waste site.

Another strategy is to buy the cheapest home in the best neighborhood. The bigger and more lavish houses on each side of yours will appreciate yours just by association. If you do move in, though, don't expect any *other* kind of association with your new neighbors, as they will be mad as heck that your house is there at all, because it is depreciating *their* properties.

If you put up new siding and give your new home a general face-lift and landscape makeover, using sweat equity (physical labor), you should improve your chances of being invited to the next July 4th neighborhood barbecue, and you will definitely improve your chances of making a profit when reselling.

## Playing Sherlock Holmes

Every home has problems, and an anxious seller may not be motivated to share every little flaw or idiosyncrasy of the home with you as you both sit down to sign the final papers. Though the seller may be required by law to disclose a host of potential problems—even if doing so may change a buyer's mind—proving you were deceived *after* the fact may be difficult. You must learn to be a scrutinizing buyer.

Wet basements, for example, are a common problem. Visiting homes only during thunderstorms or during the Spring rainy season will sniff out those leaks easily. (Snorkeling equipment in each room is another clue.)

Tiny piles of sawdust in corners may indicate termites or other unfriendlies—not the harmless result of the toddler bringing in sand from the backyard, as the seller may have suggested.

Always check the basic structure, the foundation and the roof. Ceiling jackposts in every room are not a good sign.

Improper wiring can be creatively hidden by hanging Chinese lanterns or Christmas tree bulbs from loose wires. All Christmas tree decorations should be down by June, no matter how sincere the seller's excuses seem.

You should make any purchase agreement contingent upon an independent appraisal and construction inspection by a firm of your choice. An independent inspection is worth the few extra dollars when you are contemplating the single largest purchase of your life.

Home inspections, property surveys, certified termite and other pest inspections in certain geographical climates, and a real estate attorney who can alter a purchasing contract in your interest, are all allies you cannot afford to overlook. Homebuyers tend to forget that everone else—seller, real estate agent, and lender—has a vested interest in moving property. But only *you* have to live with any mistakes you make in this area.

## 'Tis The Season To House Hunt

*When* you choose to house hunt is more important than you think. The more competitors for each home there are, the more likely the buyer will insist on top dollar for a property. Most buyers house hunt in the Spring and Summer when there is lots of built-in competition. The simple rules of supply and demand work in those seasons. The more buyers for a home, the better for the seller and the poorer the negotiating position of the potential buyer.

(In a *seller's market,* there are more buyers than homes available. In a *buyer's market,* the opposite is true.

If you are a seller, you want hoards of prospective buyers beating a path to your door. But if you are a buyer, taking a number and standing in line to view a home is far from optimal.)

The best time to buy may be Winter. A certain percentage of homeowners are always in transit from one area to another. A job transfer, a change in financial status, unemployment, a family death, or a change in health may force a seller to move quickly in an off-season.

Winter is also a good time to look for distress sales. You won't have to stand in line in -20° weather to wait for a hungry seller to let you in. You may, however, need enough identification to prove you are not an outpatient at the local sanitarium if you track down a home in January, especially in a northern climate.

The length of time a home has been on the market will also expose a potential bargain. If your real estate agent is not cooperative when you request to see all listings that have been on the market for a year or more, you may be able to spot these gems by yourself. Look for rusty "For Sale" signs, cobwebs over the front door, and a welcome that makes you wonder if you have just won the lottery.

The longer a home has been listed, the more negotiable the price becomes. Don't be afraid to bid well below the asking price, though $99.99 *is* an insulting first offer. A seller will not advertise he is desperate to move. But if you are a good poker player, you should be able to assess a seller's situation and ferret out the truly desperate.

Don't think of this new home as your final nest or you will tend to overbuy and purchase more home than you originally anticipated. Stick by your original estimates. It is not your obligation to understand the seller's situation and why he must receive more out of the home you are considering.

(I know of one devious young man whose grandmother died so many times he had to change jobs just to keep up that sympathy tactic.)

For best results, deal with more than one agent. Don't be coerced into a bidding war with another buyer. There is always another deal around the corner. This is a decision that will affect you for many years. Buy with your head, not your heart.

## What About Sales & Auctions?

I am frequently asked about bank foreclosures and sheriff sales. These can be bargains but can also trap an unwary buyer into an unwanted purchase. There may be no opportunity to inspect the home or view the interior of a property on the auction block, and any purchase is considered final.

If you later discover the home is sliding down the scenic hillside it was constructed on, is located under an airline flyway, or is slowly sinking into the sunset due to an underground river or quicksand, it will be impossible to unload it onto another unsuspecting buyer—you will be forced to disclose the negative facts that were unknown to you when you purchased. In general, these types of sales should not be attempted by the public.

## Making An Offer They Can't Refuse

Once you have found your new home, you will have to make an offer. This is where the women are separated from the boys. One friendly reminder: Do you remember the last time you made a first offer on a car, a boat, a stereo, or piece of furniture, and the seller grabbed it like he had been told beforehand what was behind Door #3? I'll bet you still remember the empty feeling in the pit of your stomach that immediately told you had offered too much.

Bidding and counterbidding are part of the Money Game. Do not be afraid to offer less than the agent told you the seller would accept. The owner wants the most he can get for his home. The agent is working for the seller and for his or her commission, which is a percentage of the final sale price. You are virtually on your own when it comes to the final stretch—you can always go up; you can never come down. This is no time to worry about your image. It is far better to haggle like an Armenian rug merchant than to get the seller to like you—by paying him more than he ever thought he could get.

All conditions and costs in purchasing real estate are negotiable. Don't be led into paying for extras because you are told that "the buyer *always* shoulders that charge."

## My Lawyer's Bigger Than Yours

You should engage a good real estate attorney from the beginning. The contracts you will eventually sign have been written by lawyers who were *not* paid by you. You'd better have someone on your side.

If an agent or lender attempts to talk you out of consulting with legal counsel, ignore them. Why don't they want you to have a lawyer? Because lawyers are also known as "deal-killers," which certainly makes them sound like the kind of pros *I* want to go into battle with.

## Tips, Tips, More Tips

If possible, try to time your transaction to coincide with low interest rates—3% would be ideal, but I doubt you can outwait the market that long.

Make your purchase agreement subject to every condition you can think of—financing, locking in a specified interest rate, a completion date if the home is newly built, required dates of occupancy, health permits if necessary, survey results, FHA or VA requirements, the absence of any encumbrances or liens on the property, and the adjustment of taxes, water, and other prorated bills that may become issues later.

If you are selling one home and buying another, never, *never,* **never** allow the new buyers to move into your old home before the transaction has closed and the deed transferred. Until the purchasing deal is completed, you are still the legal owner. If the buyer finds a problem with the home, changes his or her mind, or has other problems, the deal may collapse. If the buyer's lawyer has been aggressive enough to add escape clauses to the purchasing contract, the buyer may walk away before the transaction has been completed without owing you one thin dime. If the home burns down or a liability problem arises, *you* are still responsible.

If you are forced to allow a buyer to rent for a brief period of time—perhaps because his house has sold and his furniture is out in the street—you may stipulate that the buyer pay a small stipend for monthly rent until the deal is consummated. And think you were being awfully smart.

If so, you have just invited someone, at your expense, to spend the winter in your home at bargain rates. During which, of course, the closing process languishes because the buyer has lost all motivation to take possession, start paying larger house payments and take over the taxes, insurance and other maintenance costs.

There is a way to avoid this: If your lawyer has added a rental clause of $800, $1,000 or $1,500 per month—not a "small stipend" by anyone's standards—the buyer will be much more motivated to help you, the bank and his wallet by completing the deal as soon as possible.

Plan to get sick one hour after you have signed the closing documents—it's called *buyer's remorse,* the result of suddenly recognizing the enormity of what you have done. It is a common malady, so don't attempt to filch the mortgage papers from the lender's or real estate broker's office later that night.

If you have followed all of the rules outlined in this book, you have made the best possible decisions and the best possible deal.

## chapter eleven

# Funding College: For Martyrs Only

---

*Live long enough to become a burden to your children!*
—My favorite current bumper sticker

This chapter is primarily written for parents who are ready and willing to sacrifice their own self-interest to provide their children with the tools and skills they desperately need in today's technological world. It also has a message for children who don't want their parents to go bankrupt in the process and retire as wards of the state.

Surviving your child's college years is the ultimate trial by fire. As a parent who has much (too much!) experience on the subject, I promise you that the cost of your child's chosen alma mater will be inversely proportional to the size of your college fund.

No matter how empty you may feel waving goodbye to your college frosh, reminding him or her to call home often, you will soon learn to shudder at the ring of the telephone. Why? Because most conversations go something like this (what your student says followed in parentheses by what your student *really means*):

> "Hi, Mom. I've been thinking about you." (*I just spent my last five dollars and have tapped everyone else I know for a loan.*)

"How are you feeling?" *(Is this the best time to hit you up for money?)*

"I've been so busy studying, I haven't had time to call or write." *(I remembered you immediately upon running out of cash.)*

"The food here is not fit to eat, and they serve such small portions." *(I spent $50 in 30 days on pizza and junk food.)*

"But don't worry, there's a grocery store close by." *(My mother would never allow me to starve—she spent my whole childhood making me clean my plate.)*

"I've been hoping to join a fraternity/sorority because it gets lonely without you, but I can't afford it." *(I could become a social outcast. Besides, wouldn't fraternity/sorority dues be cheaper than coming to visit me so often?)*

"I would *really* love to come home for Thanksgiving, but I don't have the money." *(You wouldn't be able to eat one bite of turkey knowing I was the only human being on campus, would you?)*

"Boy, are books expensive! I started this extra research project but the lab fees cost a bundle." *(If I never win the Nobel prize, it could be because you deprived me of a few test tubes.)*

"I sent you a birthday card because I didn't have the money to call. Did you get it?" *(I've got to get to the store immediately and pick one up.)*

"I can't talk too long because all the other kids have their own phones, and I'm talking from one of my friend's rooms." *(I could call you more often if I had my own phone. And they can even arrange to just include it on your regular bill. Cool, huh?)*

"The weather is getting colder, but I think I can manage with my old jacket if I wear enough sweaters underneath." *(Everybody else bought a neat leather jacket.)*

"I have to go now because I want to be well rested for tomorrow's classes." *(The dorm party is starting.)*

"The other moms have sent goody boxes so I don't need anything." *(I'm just piling on a little more guilt before I hit you with the punch line.)*

"By the way, could you spare a few dollars extra this month—for the research project, remember?" (No translation necessary.)

There was a time, somewhen shrouded in mist, that my offspring asked for amounts that at least bore some relationship to my checkbook balance. After several years of paying for medical and law school, I have no sympathy for the politicians trying to solve our national budget deficit. I have solved one of my own.

If you are raising a professional, you are unquestionably very proud. When he or she actually walks down the graduation aisle, you will temporarily forget the agony and the compromises you have made to see this day. In the meantime, you will also forget what steak tastes like, what a new car smells like, and what your doctor and dentist look like. Take a lot of pictures on Graduation Day—they will be the most costly you ever shot!

## They Should At Least Name A Dorm For You

If you were sending your student to college right now, you could count on paying old Boola Boola U. $6,000 a year. That's for tuition, room and board, and minimal fees.

There is no "fat" in this number—no pizzas, airline tickets home (or trip money for interviews for graduate school), clothing expenditures, and no reserves for car expenses, insurance, gasoline, and telephone bills.

And college costs are escalating even as you read this chapter. Every school of higher learning lives within the same constraints that you do. There are utilities, overhead, salaries, costs for expansion and upkeep, supplies, and innovative equipment the college needs to remain competitive with all the other colleges. All of which can cost big bucks.

What does this mean in terms of future costs? The following chart shows what you can expect to pay a four-year school if your son or daughter is ready for college somewhere during the next 20 years, with three possible levels of inflation—6%, 8% and 10%.

| Year | 6% | 8% | 10% |
|------|------|------|------|
| 1995 | 35,126 | 38,567 | 42,273 |
| 2000 | 47,006 | 56,667 | 68,081 |
| 2005 | 62,904 | 83,263 | 109,644 |
| 2010 | 84,081 | 122,341 | 176,583 |

Remember: These are costs for a *state-supported* university or college! If you and your student are considering a private school or specialized institution, *double* or *triple* the above figures.

## Who's Paying For That Degree?

Does your student need financial aid? Every parent I know can respond with an honest and resounding "YES!" But what *you* think you can afford to pay old Boola Boola may bear little resemblance to *their* calculations of your "fair share" of your son's or daughter's four-year ivy-covered experience. If you are counting on a mixed menu of grants, scholarships, loans, and tax incentives to bolster your small amount of personal savings, dream on.

Unless your child is valedictorian at a large school where scholarships abound, does exceptionally well on the SAT or ACT, or is a top athlete, scholarships will probably be few and relatively small. The affluent and the indigent have the best chance of attending the college of their choice ...and being able to pay for it.

All your tangible, intangible and personal assets will be factored into a formula when you request financial aid. In essence, the more responsibly you have lead your life, the more you will be penalized by the present system of allotting financial aid. If you have been able to put away some savings, you will be expected to turn them over. Your student will be expected to work each and every summer, with all earnings counted as college resources. He or she will be expected to enroll in a campus work-study program for eight to twelve hours a week...and probably still need a student loan.

The myth that the government or a university will understand that you have house payments, car payments, credit card debts and other obligations will quickly disappear when they inform you just how little, er, much, they plan to offer you in financial aid.

If you are a middle-income family, you will be expected to shoulder most of the cost by yourself. A family income of $30,000 or more will separate you from most of the college entitlement programs and federal and state subsidy grant programs. Depending on family size and the number of children dependent on you or also attending college, that figure will change slightly...but not enough to forestall a quick dash to the medicine cabinet.

## Tomorrow Is Too Late To Start

Given the rapid rise in college costs expected over the next 20 years, the most serious mistake you can make is waiting too long to start your college fund. If you have just had a new baby, *now* is the time to start. The more time your college fund has to compound and work, the greater the amount that will be available, the less you will need to dip into hard-earned retirement dollars.

If you've already started your college fund, make sure the return you are receiving is sufficient.

College costs generally have outpaced the return on bonds and are expected to continue to do so. (There are few, if any, 10-12% bonds around that *I* know of.)

Pre-paid tuition plans have also been a failure to date because inflation has outpaced the promised lump sum benefits. With costs increasing from 8% to 10% annually, you must re-think your investment strategy. Those "safe" government bonds and your passbook savings account (earning 5%?) aren't likely to achieve your long-term college goals.

Don't be misled by promoters and marketers who claim they can ferret out unclaimed scholarships or magically show you methods of sending your child to school almost free. These schemes may involve leveraging your home or purchasing questionable products.

College planning is not an area where you should be performing self-taught surgery. Spend time with a financial planning professional—calculate the approximate costs of a four-year college when your student will be ready to attend and the general rate of return you need to earn to cover them. Do *not* seek advice only from a marketer or a salesman, whose primary objective lies in getting your signature on the dotted line. If you cannot seem to part with a few dollars to get some objective advice, visit a number of financial enterprises and research your options before taking off in any one direction.

Always remember: Over the long term, you *must* beat inflation. The longer the time horizon to your goal, the greater fluctuation your principal can handle. The shorter the time horizon, the less fluctuation your principal can take. The older you are, the more conservative your investment philosophies may be. If you stash your money in guaranteed accounts because you fear losing any of your principal, inflation will make sure you lose anyway.

In this instance, there is no such thing as "safe" or "riskless." No matter what you do, you are going to have to take some risk. The solution is to learn how to *manage* that risk. In one word, that means "diversify." When investing in real estate, the three keys are "location, location and location." When you work your money, the magic method is "diversification, diversification, diversification."

The best solutions combine a variety of strategies with enough time to let compound interest do some of the work. Since this is one of those circumstances when you need a fixed amount of money within a fixed amount of time, there are only two ways to create the totals you need: (1) provide enough original seed dollars so you can live with lower returns or (2) find a way to increase the rate of return on those investable dollars you have.

There are many options available for college funding— Series EE bonds, zero coupon bonds timed to mature when needed (not later because that increases interest rate risk), money markets, mutual funds with conservative philosophies, even more aggressive funds utilizing strategies such as dollar cost averaging.

Any combination of these may be an ideal mix of return and risk management that will work for you. The amount of time is critical in the choice of financial vehicles. If you are not totally familiar with these options, get to the library or start reading one or more of the personal money management magazines on the newsstands.

## What If Tomorrow's Already Here?

If college is only a few years away and you failed to set up an inflation-beating college fund 10 or 20 years ago, there are some crisis methods you can employ. These options should be used *only* after careful thought and research:

1)  Home equity loans
2)  National Direct Student Loans
3)  Guaranteed Student Loans
4)  Borrowing against life insurance cash values
5)  Refinancing a home mortgage
6)  Loans from an employee retirement plan
7)  Terminating an employee retirement fund
8)  Loans against a stock or bond portfolio
9)  Enrolling in a military program such as ROTC
10) Cooperative education
11) Company-sponsored education
12) Commuting to a local school

***Borrowing on the equity in your home*** seems more attractive in today's tax climate, but it is also a potentially dangerous solution. You are risking putting your home on the auction block. With changing interest rates and the popularity of adjustable rate mortgages, you could find, in a few short years, that your payments are priced above your budget.

Use this solution sparingly. Most parents do not have many years to plan for retirement after paying for college and should be salting money away for when *they* need it, not struggling to pay off a second mortgage so Junior can attend Ivy U.

***National Direct Student Loans*** offer a limited amount of borrowing power and seem more viable because the student can ultimately take on the repayment responsibility. But be careful—defaulting on these loans is no longer tolerated.

***Guaranteed Student Loans*** are granted through individual banking and lending institutions. Limits vary and must be discussed with individual lenders. Give yourself enough time for loan processing—like most governmental programs, they take time to complete. Applying six to nine months before the funds are needed is not too early. The first time will be the most confusing. After that, the forms will become easier to complete and process.

***Cash value life insurance policies*** can be borrowed against. Just remember that you are *decreasing* the amount of your insurance coverage at a time when your liabilities may be *increasing*. Instead, consider surrendering your cash value policies to free up your insurance savings, purchasing term insurance to cover your present needs, and using what's left over to invest in a college fund. Then, as soon as your student graduates from college, reduce the amount of your term coverage by the amount you would have needed for college if you had died, and put the difference of the premium into your own retirement investment plans or increase your employer retirement plan contribution.

My advice from an earlier chapter was to purchase term insurance early, while your family is growing, grab your cash value, and invest it elsewhere. If you followed that advice, you will not need to risk decreasing your insurance coverage and won't have to pay an insurance company interest to borrow your own money. You will simply withdraw it from your own accounts when needed.

***Refinancing a home mortgage*** may be helpful if interest rates have significantly decreased since your original mortgage date. If interest rates have increased or remained stable, this method may not be wise.

Refinancing is most beneficial when interest rates have moved down at least two percentage points and you can recover the cost and expenses of the refinancing in less than two years. If you do not intend to remain in your present home for several years, refinancing is probably not a good alternative.

***Borrowing from an employee retirement plan*** may be allowed, but the government is becoming more protective of individual money set aside for retirement and has

clearly indicated that it intends to be less liberal about
letting people tap those funds. By the time you need college
money, there may be no legal methods of tapping the
source.

And remember: You are robbing your retirement fund
and will have to replace whatever money you borrowed,
*plus interest.* Therefore, you are obligating yourself to
*more* debt, which is usually not the most prudent solution.

***Terminating an employee retirement plan*** may be even
less attractive. In the above example, even though you are
borrowing your own money, at least you must pay yourself
back. Unless you possess great financial discipline, this
option is not recommended, even though you won't need to
pay back the money you took out.

If you are seriously considering this alternative, your
previous savings record is already suspect, and your savings attitudes must change immediately and dramatically
to replace the funds in some alternative way. Otherwise,
the net result will be that you have wiped out your retirement savings and not given yourself enough time to
replace these vitally needed dollars.

***Borrowing against securities*** can be effective, but if you
have stocks and bonds laying around, why not just sell
them? This solution may be a more viable option for the
IBM executive than for the average college parent who's
already considering selling off the family pet in order to
save the weekly cost of dog food.

***The military*** (all three branches) have attractive programs to fund an education. These are popular, but there
are service stipulations attached. I would advise a student
to explore each service branch with an open mind to discover the various options. Some programs allow full education prior to enlistment. Others accumulate a college
fund for a student to use to attend college, but only after
his or her discharge.

The likelihood of a student receiving an education will
be greater if he or she goes directly to college from high

school, rather than waiting until his or her military commitment is finished. After leaving high school, life offers so many distractions that there is a tendency to detour from the original educational goal. Additionally, the older student may be reluctant to enroll in a school where the majority of other students are so much younger.

***Cooperative education*** can solve an otherwise impossible situation. The benefit lies in the self-funding style of the education—the student works part-time and attends class part-time. The work is coordinated with the curriculum of study so sufficient income can be generated to maintain the costs of attending school.

The major disadvantages of cooperative education lie in the length of time it takes to graduate. A typical four-year course is often stretched to six years or more. The student must also be dedicated enough to pursue the longer time frame. But for a persistent student with few other options, this can work out nicely.

***Some companies offer tuition-paid college courses*** to high school graduates/employees as an incentive to improve employee productivity and performance. These classes are often conducted during working hours. The company may, however, stipulate some type of reciprocal agreement, such as the student's promise to work for them for a certain period of time after his or her education is completed.

***Commuting to a local college*** may decrease the total college experience from a social standpoint, but from a purely financial aspect, it may need to be considered. There are hidden costs to consider even in this option—a car, gasoline, insurance, maintenance, lunches, parking fees, and the cost of maintaining a student at home. These must be compared with the increased cost of room and board on campus.

However these costs compare, one advantage of commuting remains: If a student has not matured to the point that he or she can handle the freedom and lack of guidelines in a college environment, this may be a temporary solution. It is better for a student to successfully complete his or her first year of college even if somewhat tied to home than to drop out because he or she lacked the self-discipline to handle that critical first year.

## For The Truly Desperate

If further creative solutions are necessary, you might consider the following list:

1) Disown your child—after two years he or she will be considered an independent student and treated on the basis of his or her own assets;

2) Marry off your child before college age—you will achieve the same result as above;

3) Market your child to colleges as unique—it may be easier to receive scholarships as an Egyptian Art major than as a Biology major;

4) Transfer all your assets to someone else (you can trust) to appear as poor as possible;

5) Dissolve your marriage temporarily—have your teenager live with the poorest parent;

6) Become a workaholic and convince yourself you have three jobs and work 100 hours a week because you *really* enjoy it;

7) Find an affluent benefactor and convince him or her to send your child to college by explaining that contributions on the child's behalf, made directly to the college, are not subject to gift taxes.

## Get Your Student Involved

I have encountered both types of parents—those determined to fund the entire cost of higher education for their children and those not willing to contribute 39¢ to their child's schooling. My tendency lies somewhere in the middle: A child who has no responsibility for the sacrifices involved in funding his or her college education tends to view the sacrifices of the parents less reverently.

Encourage (or require) your child to work before college and during summers away from school, to participate in work-study campus programs during the school year, and to take over the responsibility for repaying student loans after graduation. After all, at that point, his or her liabilities should still be quite a bit less than yours!

Planning your child's education does not mean throwing some money toward the goal, crossing your fingers, and hoping (against hope!) that things will work out. It takes "X" amount of money working at "Y" rate of return, compounded for "Z" years, to create the total you need. You must know the amount of seed dollars ("X") necessary to create your "pot of gold," the combined rate of return you must receive annually to achieve your ends ("Y"), the inflation factors to include, and the final totals necessary to satisfy your needs.

Settling for any less than all of the above information is akin to getting in your car and starting out to drive from Los Angeles to New York with no map and no route in mind. If you manage to arrive at all, it will be due to sheer luck.

And you will undoubtedly be too late.

## chapter twelve

# The Golden Years: Why Are They Tarnishing?

Some day one of the following will occur:

(1) You will die;

(2) You will become disabled;

(3) You will be asked by your company to retire; or

(4) You will want to turn over and go back to sleep when the morning alarm rings... and retire voluntarily.

If you die first, this chapter will benefit your spouse or help to create an estate for your heirs. If, however, you actually live long enough to retire, using the advice in this chapter may separate you from the rest of your generation —the largest generation that ever grew old—by ensuring you have enough money to live on when you do retire.

There is no great secret to retirement planning. If you spend everything today, you will have nothing left for tomorrow. And if you owe it all to yourself now, you may be living out of an appliance carton on some suburban curbside in your old age. If you are paying for your neighbor-impressing status with a huge mortgage and inflated lifestyle, those "Golden Years" may start tarnishing awfully quickly.

I won't bore you with statistics because they just don't frighten people anymore into planning for retirement. Everyone thinks he or she won't be one of the unlucky victims. People don't actively plan to fail in later life; they simply fail to plan.

People used to retire, live a few years afterward, then die, leaving only a spouse to frugally spend whatever remained. Today most of us are not as ready to disappear so quickly after our working lives have wound down. But if we hope and expect to live longer, we have to provide money to make that happen.

Retirement planning isn't a topic that comes up around the neighborhood pool. It is depressing to admit one will get wrinkles and arthritis and live long enough to become ill more often before dying. It's much more fun to plan next year's vacation, the purchase of a new car, the addition to the house, or the new pool and sauna.

All those weeks, months and years of free spending will suddenly add up to a lifetime of not saving. Then your attitude will definitely change. A year or two before retirement, you will realize that you are in big financial trouble. Without enough resources, you will look around for someone to bail you out.

## Who *Won't* Be There For You

Years ago the government had an idea—to tax current workers to help out elderly former workers, who wouldn't live very long anyway. And there were so many workers out there! Heck. They figured out they could continue this kind of clever money hokus pocus *ad infinitum*. Social security (that's what they called it) benefit payments would only be a supplement to the elderly, widows, orphans and disabled workers, a little extra.

Problem #1: They didn't count on the Baby Boom, among other demographic shifts, which has led to fewer and fewer workers supporting more and more retirees.

Problem #2: The elderly forgot to notice the fine prin<
about this just being supplemental. For far too many
Social Security benefits became the major, if not the sole
money they received after retirement.

Problem #3: Despite whatever you've heard about th<
"surplus" in the system, I wouldn't count on Social Secur
ity to even buy the week's groceries by the time I retire: No
even the government can tax the half of the populatio:
(that will be working) heavily enough to feed the other hal
(that will be retired, disabled or indigent).

But then, why worry? The government has all bu
eliminated age discrimination and mandatory retiremen
from the workplace. What a victory! Now you can worl
right up to the day you die.

## Uncle Sam Wants You To Spend, Spend, Spend

The government has also decided it should shoulde:
the responsibility for keeping the economy growing (or, a'
least, *looking* that way). Unfortunately, this urge has pu
them in direct conflict with your responsibility for retire
ment planning: If you save or invest every penny you car
get your hands on, that's good for you. But if everyone
saves all their money, too few dollars will remain fo:
spending on cars and houses and vacations. The economy
will slow down.

You can appreciate the government's dilemma: I<
*knows* it can't provide all of the money you will need tc
retire. Congress also realizes if it motivates you to save toc
much, economic growth will stagnate and recession coulc
set in, and every politician knows that a recession is dead
ly to a politician's career.

So Uncle Sam, while moaning about our low rate of
savings (not like those Japanese), usually does the exac'
opposite—sacrificing long-term planning for short-term
solutions and political expediency.

The IRA, for example, was heralded by everyone as a terrific savings gimmick. *But it worked too well. People saved too much.* Once the government saw how many billions of dollars were flooding into IRAs—and not into consumer goods or to fund Congressional pork barrel projects—they performed major surgery on it.

So, for most of us, contributions to an IRA are no longer tax deductible. How did we respond to the government's high-handed flip flop? Exactly as Uncle Sam hoped—by once more spending our way to instant gratification and happiness. Legislators solved their short-term problem at the expense of a long-term impending disaster. Americans are spending money they should be putting toward their futures, tax coffers are decreasing anyhow, and the retirement problem is shelved and repressed by everyone.

Ignorance is NOT bliss.

## Widget Inc. Is Like My Family

If the government isn't working on the retirement problem, and we aren't saving enough ourselves, just who is going to make sure we don't all starve to death? Obviously, employers will have to shoulder the added responsibility, right?

Wrong! Company executives are at least as smart as politicians, and they are staying up at night figuring ways to avoid being forced to increase pension benefits. (Most of them are also trying to find ways to dip into "over-funded" pension plans so they can use the money for *their* short-term needs.)

## The Bottom Line

Promised retirement funds will come from your company pension (if it is still solvent), subsidized by some Social Security (if it is still there for the middle class). *The remainder of retirement funding is your responsibility.* So a combination of personal investments had better be working harder than inflation to keep up. Like Alice in Wonderland, your money has to work faster and faster for you to stay in the same place and retain the same purchasing power in the face of inflation.

Ever notice how things you buy are getting smaller and smaller? Candy bars, bottles of pop, loaves of bread, the dollar bill? The American dream house has become a dream condo and may even become a dream closet or a dream cardboard box in the future. (The only things you can count on expanding over the years are your waistline and those adjustable mortgage house payments.)

You don't have to be a chicken to recognize an egg, only to lay one. And you are going to lay a whopper if you expect retirement to take care of itself.

## Numbers Can Lie...Convincingly

If I told you that to retire at age 65 on $30,000 a year and be sure you have the same amount of money until you reach 85, you would need a lump sum of $280,948 continually working at 10% per year after taxes (a combination of your company pension, Social Security benefits, and your own retirement investments), you might feel quite comfortable. That number seems attainable.

That number is also a fantasy using the same kind of faulty arithmetic you get when salespeople talk to you about their retirement planning programs.

Those calculations have totally disregarded the ravaging effects of inflation after retirement. Can you still buy ground beef for 33¢ a pound like in the '60s? How about a luxury car for $5,000 as in the early '70s? Or a budget hotel room for $12 per night as in the early '80s?

When we factor in the effects of inflation at 6% per year after retirement (and pretend it will never be higher), the numbers are a little different—you will need to save

$431,829 by your retirement date to have $30,000 a year *after inflation.*

Okay, your blood pressure is beginning to rise, but you can still see how you can save enough to provide that pot of gold before you retire.

Unfortunately, I've fooled you once more. This sleight-of-hand trick deceives you into believing that $1.00 today is still going to be worth $1.00 when you retire. Is inflation going to take a vacation while you build up your retirement fund?

If you are now 45 and have decided you will need $30,000 per year worth of *purchasing power* at age 65, that $30,000 in 1990 dollars will have to become $96,214 in inflated dollars! (So much for early retirement.). In other words, to retain the same lifestyle that $30,000 will buy today, it will take $96,214 in 20 years...and 6% more every year thereafter.

You had better sit down for this: To get this kind of money, you will need to accumulate a total of $1,384,934 in future inflated dollars in vested benefits from your pension, Social Security and your own investments or you will reduce your lifestyle below what $30,000 will buy today. Most people I know ALREADY believe that $30,000 is a reduced lifestyle.

How close will *you* be to the astronomical number above? Using the Rule of 72, you can calculate just how close the money you expect at retirement will come to what you will need. If money is working at a rate of 6% per year, it will double every twelve years. Inflation can be calculated on a reverse basis: If inflation averages 6% a year, twelve years from now that money will be worth only *one half* of what it is today—$30,000 today will have the purchasing power of $15,000 in twelve years. In another twelve years, that $15,000 will buy only $7,500 in goods and needed services.

For a quick overview of all your expected retirement benefits, calculate the amounts you expect at age 65 from

Social Security, your pension plan at work, any other qualified retirement plans, your insurance policy retirement
plans and annuities, and your retirement investments.
Then divide their value to you at retirement in half for
every twelve years you have *until* retirement age.

If Social Security, for example, promises you $600 per
month ($7,200 per year) at retirement, in twelve years the
purchasing power will have decreased to $3,600 per year.
In another twelve years that value will become $1,200 per
year.

It shouldn't take you long to realize that the financial
institutions that have promised that their products will
make you comfortable at retirement have *not* been telling
you the whole truth. If you don't start cutting out more of
the financial middlemen and getting involved in researching some options of your own, even that cardboard box
won't be affordable when you retire.

## Think You've Got Me?

If you think you can retire on much less than today's
income because you won't have a mortgage or dependent
children, you are ignoring the elderly around you. You
will still need 65-75% of today's income—like an older
home, you will also need upkeep.

Your dentist won't fill cavities anymore; instead, she'll
prescribe a new mouthful of teeth.

You will no longer have a job, so there will be no more
raises.

You will live on a fixed pension, only a portion of your
previous salary, begin to get sick, and pay $100 to $200 a
month or more for prescriptions. You may well lose your
employer health benefits entirely and have to fund health
care above Medicare-type programs yourself.

Most of your present overhead will continue—rising
insurance premiums, new car prices, and other costs that
don't stop when the mortgage does.

Along with other surprises you haven't anticipated, tax rates will likely be *higher* than today. $30,000 a year is not a lot of money, even in today's dollars.

A nursing home won't think so either if you need custodial care. With costs of $2,000 per month or more, even one spouse can quickly bankrupt a retired couple. What will you do then? Sell off a bathroom or an extra bedroom so you can purchase groceries or prescriptions?

Some people believe they will retire in a lower tax bracket. In fact, that is one benefit prominently advertised by IRA sellers—IRA funds will accumulate tax-deferred until you receive them after retirement, when you will be taxed at a lower rate because you will be earning less money.

I have a news flash for you: Since most folks can't live on what they make today, you had better NOT retire in a lower tax bracket. If you do, that means that you will be even *more* broke that you are now!

We have seen the lowest tax rates in history, but "read my lips" *can't* last forever. Congress will have to eventually raise taxes. You could very well retire in a *higher* tax bracket than today, even if your income remains constant from now until retirement age.

This is the time to take a more serious approach to retirement and reposition your assets to work harder for you. Once you understand the devastating effects of inflation and the time value of money, you will be equipped to defend your hard-earned dollars.

## So What Do You Do?

The word "safe" rarely appears in my vocabulary. Because in financial planning, ***there is no such thing as "risk-free" or safe.***

When you strive for higher returns, you usually encounter greater risk.

If all your money sits in a low-yielding, "guaranteed" account, you risk the continuous loss of principal through inflation.

Risk is everywhere, whether it is market risk, business risk, financial risk, or inflation risk. The secret is to understand each type of risk and learn to manage them through diversification.

People often translate "diversification" to mean only that money, like eggs, should be put into several baskets. That's just part of the definition. Additionally, those baskets must be composed of different *kinds* of financial vehicles. Putting all your money into ten stocks instead of just one is not diversification—you are still subject to the risks inherent in the stock market. Lumping all your assets into CDs and guaranteed accounts subject you to inflation risk.

Today's trendy financial planning concept is "asset allocation," just a gussied-up phrase that means good, old-fashioned diversification. It uses a combination of different types of vehicles to provide a total rate of return with a manageable amount of risk.

Mixing and matching financial instruments takes a certain amount of expertise. If you decided to build a bicycle by purchasing individual parts from different manufacturers with different specifications and tolerances, numerous grades of construction, and differing standards of quality, would you have any chance of creating a machine that would actually fit together?

Unless you are a novice money manager and are willing to spend significant time on your financial life, you had better seek the advice of someone whose job it is to make sure all parts of your financial life fit well together and function according to your goals and expectations.

Whatever plan you wind up putting together should be monitored annually, and modifications should be made where needed. Those areas which have underperformed should be reevaluated for their future potential.

Build your retirement program gradually—for comfort, not for speed. Don't invest heavily in aggressive growth vehicles if you are inherently conservative and roller coasters give you nosebleeds.

Don't be impressed by the word "guaranteed." Your response to such a claim should be "guaranteed by whom?" "Guaranteed by the U. S. Government" is a little different than "guaranteed by Al's U-Drive-In Bank." If your employer (and the pension plan) disappears, a bank or S&L closes, or an insurance company decides to drop your product line, what are their guarantees worth?

If you jump into the stock market, use a long-term approach, and don't chase profits by trying to "time" the market (attempting to "buy low, sell high"). Studies have shown this approach does not work. If you take away the bulls and the bears from the market, there's a lot less manure. Bulls and bears can both make money, but pigs generally get nothing but the manure.

Always purchase quality products. Don't be attracted by securities which are so cheap that you can buy them in great quantities. A security priced at just $1.00 per share may *look* like a winner if it would just move up to $1.50. But chances are it is priced at $1.00 because that is *exactly* what it is worth (if you're lucky; if not, it's worth pennies).

Never, never give cash or other negotiable instruments to an advisor or representative who promises to make the trade or deliver your money to the investment company. Always use a cashier's check which can be traced or, at least, will have to be fraudulently cashed if someone wants to use it for a purpose other than you intended.

It is generally *not* a good idea to make checks payable to a representative or individual. Most financial professionals would not want to be associated that closely with any monetary transfers.

So if your advisor encourages you to "just make the check out to cash," they should be able to hear your alarm bells ringing all the way to Sheboygan.

## chapter thirteen

# You Can't Take It With You, But You Can Decide Who Gets It

When you hear about the "estate" someone left behind, it conjures up visions of a 100-room mansion on a few hundred more beautifully landscaped acres—with priceless rugs on every floor, Old Masters on every wall, and a wine cellar that would make most restaurants proud; a family yacht happily plying the waters between Barbados and the tip of Aruba; vaults filled with blue chip securities, family jewels and assorted heirlooms; a recent appearance on "Lifestyles of..." ...you know.

Given assets like these, it is certainly understandable why lawyers spent months, nay years, carefully directing the money, the homes, the yacht, the jewels and each and every knickknack to the loved ones left behind.

Frankly, it probably doesn't occur to most of you—whose "mansion" is overmortgaged and underfurnished, whose "yacht" is in the kid's bathtub, and whose "vaults" look curiously like piggies—that anyone, including your immediate family, would be interested in attending a reading of your will.

In fact, many of you may think being absent may be the smartest thing you ever did. Why would you want to be around when an accounting of your remaining debts determines who is responsible for coming up with the cash needed to bury you, pay final expenses, fend off a line of creditors larger than the crowds on double coupon days, and face the banker, hat (and unpaid mortgage and car loan) in hand.

Most of you probably feel your family fortune could be handled with less ceremony, considering the personal assets to be disbursed:

> I leave my overstuffed TV chair to Rover, who, through ten years of adverse possession, probably already has legal claim to it;
>
> The assorted tools I have managed to rubberband and glue back together, I leave to my son, with the stipulation that he be forced to use them in their present condition, the result of his leaving them out in the rain to rust, in the driveway to be run over, and in the neighbor's grass;
>
> To my daughter, I give, devise and bequeath all right, title and interest in the bathroom electrical outlets, the vanity mirror, the community property hairdryers, and a life estate in the bathroom in which she spent the majority of her teenage years;
>
> The list of unfinished chores, as well as the boards for the fence, the wire for the dog run, the paint for the house, and other materials for jobs I never got around to, I give to anyone willing to haul them away and sweep up afterwards;
>
> To my grandson I leave the pool table that I saved for through the years, along with every divot, popsicle stain, and torn piece of felt that resulted from his visits;
>
> To the colony of wasps under the eaves that I could never convince to relocate, I leave my collection of pesticides and bug bombs. Because you have survived and

multiplied, evolving into a Super Race impervious to Man's designs, I believe such a strong survival instinct should be rewarded;

Finally, my touring bike, like new because I had so little time to ride it, I give to absolutely NO ONE because it's mine...mine... mine...! And I intend to do everything in my power to come back and enjoy it, without the constant worries of bills to pay, budgets to juggle, a job to hate, kids to raise, a spouse addicted to the phrase "charge it," and neighbors who, like me, spent their entire summers cultivating, fertilizing, weeding, thatching and encouraging a postage stamp of green just so we could spend every Saturday mowing off its head in order to repeat the entire inane process the following week.

## How Wrong It Can Get

My parents were considered middle-income and lived a relatively normal life. My father died, leaving a will which gave everything to my mother, Soon after, my mother passed away, also with a will, leaving her estate to her two minor children, my brother and me. Since we were minors, she established a guardianship with a judge, a family friend.

It wasn't long before the old judge died and my brother and I became wards of another judge, this time one appointed by the court. No one in my family had ever heard of this one.

Under the supposed benevolent protection and guidance of the court, strangers took total control of everything my parents had expected to pass on to us—and our home, cars, bank accounts, and all personal property were liquidated and disbursed. And not to us.

The only assets that either of us have today are two figurines, a train set, two books belonging to my father, and a small piece of cut glass that some auctioneer overlooked.

We were too young to understand everything that went on, but I can still remember that our home, which the executor demanded be liquidated, was sold for a depressed price, then re-sold within two weeks to a neighbor for more than twice its original liquidation value. Two teenagers were left to fend for themselves.

Am I stronger today for the experience? Probably. Would I recommend this plan of action to another family? Not on your life!

## Why Even *You* Need A Will

Estate planning for the yachtless is a vital part of *every* financial plan if:

1) You are married;
2) You are divorced;
3) You are widowed;
4) You have children;
5) You own tangible assets (cars, home, personal property);
6) You owe debts or financial obligations;
7) You own liquid assets (e.g., CDs, bank accounts, etc.);
8) You have intangible assets (securities, bonds, etc.);
9) You have a company pension plan of any kind;
10) You have recently bought or sold a substantial asset;
11) You own property or personal assets in another state;

12) Your financial circumstances have changed;
13) Your health has recently changed;
14) Your personal life has significantly changed
15) You intend to disinherit any of your family;
16) You may become disabled or mentally incompetent;
17) Your plan has not been updated for several years, especially since 1981;
18) Estate tax laws have changed;
19) You care who gets your property after you are gone;
20) You will eventually die.

## What A Will Does For You

A thoughtfully planned will can accomplish several things. Is it a simplistic solution to all simple estate planning? No.

A will can provide fair and equitable distribution of assets, establish a limitation on estate creditors, and help you control distribution of your property after death. It may not do this cheaply or quickly. And, despite your best intentions, wills can be contested.

### Why You Need A Lawyer

My knowledge of specific areas of law (estate planning, risk management, and investments) is not to be scoffed at. But I doubt any Bar Association would engage me for anything more serious than an intense game of billiards.

Because I am not a lawyer, this chapter makes no attempt to give legal advice or provide information that should be discussed with a competent attorney (preferably over lunch so that so that you can get a free consultation). But since estate planning is an integral part of everyone's total financial picture, this chapter *will* give you the basic data you need before meeting with your lawyer.

A competent attorney should spend enough time with you to outline all options and explore will substitutes for property ownership and distribution. Attorneys don't make a lot drafting simple wills. Their turn comes when someone dies, the family finds the will with the attorney's name clearly typed on the cover, and that attorney is instructed to initiate probate proceedings. A hefty fee for probating personal assets plus legal costs incurred may be extracted—money your family will never receive.

Just remember: The most dangerous mistake a layman can make is to assume that anyone can understand legal jargon just because the words *look* like the English language. The operative word here is "assume," which, when taken apart becomes "ass / u / me"—layman's translation, the process of making an ass out of you and me. Any connection between legalese and a layman's understanding is purely coincidental.

## How Long Can You Hold Your Financial Breath?

When you die, the probate estate will consist of those assets contained in the will or otherwise not directed under alternate forms of ownership. Bank deposits, IRAs, annuities and pensions *may* be distributed *outside* of a will so they do not have to go through probate (which, in some states, can take up to two years to distribute assets). This is one area you will want to carefully consider before lumping everything together in your will. Your attorney can work with you to explore the combination of options that will work best for you.

The following is only a partial list of alternate forms of property ownership that should be discussed: beneficiary accounts, joint and survivorship accounts, joint and survivorship property deeds, "payable on death" accounts, "Totten Trusts," joint tenants with rights of survivorship for jointly owned securities, and life insurance beneficiary clauses.

## Ensuring Insurance Proceeds

Life insurance is so often misdirected that it should be more fully discussed. The greatest advantage of a life insurance beneficiary clause is that the death benefit dollars pass directly and quickly to the named beneficiary *outside* of the will, completely avoiding probate. *If, however, life insurance policies are included in a will, they are disbursed according to the terms contained in the will ...after it has been probated.*

Wills commonly contain a clause stating that all debts are to be paid *before* the distribution of the estate's assets. If insurance policies are part of the estate's assets, this money might be open to creditor claims. Worse yet, if the estate is sued for any reason (e.g., an auto accident in which others are injured) and a claim eventually prevails upon the estate's assets, those insurance dollars could go to some stranger instead of your family.

By keeping the insurance money out of the will—which is not too difficult; just don't mention it—it cannot be attacked by creditors (other than assignees designated in the insurance policy) and a spouse cannot be forced to use it to pay any of your bills.

The primary beneficiary of an insurance policy is usually the spouse. But, in a "common disaster" (where both husband and wife die in a common accident or disaster), the insurance proceeds pass to whomever you have designated as the contingent or secondary beneficiary.

I have seen blank spaces in insurance policies where the secondary beneficiary should have been named and wasn't. If no name appears and the primary beneficiary does not survive, all death proceeds automatically revert back into the estate of the deceased and back into the will. In these situations, I have always wondered if the insurance agent's pen ran dry too soon.

If the beneficiaries are minor children, you may have a problem. No insurance company is going to write out a fat check to a four-year-old. That money will be held in some kind of trust designed by the court under a trustee named by the court.

## Let's See, Who Gets The Kids?

In many states, minors may not hold or receive property. In the event of a common disaster, if you have not designated a trustee for your minor children, the court will gladly take that little decision out of your hands. Remember how well my estate was handled.

There are many ways to spell D-I-S-A-S-T-E-R:

A relative who still has his "First Communion" money may admirably conserve the estate at all costs—even at the expense of a normal lifestyle for your children.

If the court appoints a trustee who diverts the estate's assets for his or her own benefit or simply wastes them, your children will suffer. Even if a trustee is discovered ripping off your kids (legalese: "in a breach of his fiduciary duty"), a lawsuit will be costly and time-consuming and may not recover all of the misused funds. Lastly, a court-appointed trustee may not be the person you would have chosen.

A second marriage, with or without children, really demands some serious estate planning. The blended family (his, hers and theirs) is becoming the norm today. Howard Hughes isn't the only deceased with relatives coming out of the woodwork to claim an inheritance. I have known grown children who, even before the funeral of a parent, have called to request instructions for immediately liquidating their parent's assets.

If you are smart enough to set up a legal trusteeship for your children in the case of your death, make sure you leave the trustees enough money to take care of your kids. Surprising the guardians who are suddenly responsible for raising your three kids with a $10,000 death insurance policy will *not* make them happy. Not only will your kids suffer, but so will their guardians, who will struggle to make ends meet while feeding three more kids, paying for braces and other medical expenses, clothing, school, and even college tuition. Your death insurance must be sufficient to pay off all of your liabilities plus the costs of caring for your children and any additional benefits you may wish to provide.

Unless you specify otherwise, many states direct that children receive their lump-sum inheritances at an age of majority, as early as 18 in some states. Inexpensive trusts and trust clauses in a will can be set up designating specific dates and/or events that will trigger distribution of assets to your children. An 18-year old is much more vulnerable to outside pressures to part with an inheritance than a 21-year old who has just graduated from college.

## The Taxman Always Cometh

Most of you do not have to worry about Federal estate taxes—current estate laws exempt any estate under $600,000 from them. If you and your spouse die in a common disaster, this limit doubles, to $1.2 million. But keep watching our President's lips—if these limits are lowered, you may well need to do some additional planning.

The Feds might not want you, but the *state* wants a piece of the action, and state estate taxes usually start at a much lower amount—consult your library or tax advisor to go over the estate tax tables in your state.

These estate taxes are *in addition to* any income taxes due on assets, such as pension funds, IRA accounts,

nnuities and securities. Any joint-and-survivor accounts
ill also be counted for gross estate taxes, regardless of
ny beneficiary instructions and whether or not they pass
hrough a will.

## The Work You Need To Do

Do not assume that a piece of paper, just because it has
een blessed by the legal establishment, will automatically
ccomplish your total estate objectives. I have seen wills
rinted out by office software that fall woefully short of
ddressing the unique situations of individual families.
'lanning is a compromise between deciding which
ptions are viable and which will work for you. Boilerplate
ills are only a beginning. If your attorney provides only a
implistic solution to your estate problems, you may want
o seek a second opinion.

Review all of your assets and insurance policies (even
hose at work) and determine what forms of ownership
re consistent with your present needs. Check group term
isurance policies at your job to be sure you are actually
nrolled. (Believe it or not, this has happened to more than
ne of my clients). The funeral is no time for your bereaved
pouse to discover the office secretary accidentally left your
ame off the list of group enrollees.

Check beneficiary designations on all policies (in-
luding your group policies) to be sure they are updated.
)on't expect your first spouse to hand an insurance check
o your new spouse because *you* forgot to change the bene-
ciary after the divorce. Whenever major events occur in
our life, you should examine and change your benefi-
iaries to match them.

Check group policies at work to designate both a
rimary and a contingent beneficiary (even if you have to
rite their names in the margins on the master contract).
f the office staff is not helpful, ignore their attitudes and

insist on seeing your paperwork. I doubt they would be willing to come up with the needed money for raising your family if something happened to you prematurely. Do not let anyone falsely reassure you or intimidate you out of researching in your own interest.

Income gifting techniques, lifetime gifting, trusts to avoid income as well as estate taxes, and other more complex estate solutions should be the result of a combination of an attorney's legal expertise and a tax advisor's advice. Do not expect one specialist to be equally versed in several areas. A perfectly admirable legal maneuver may cost you a bundle in additional taxes.

If you just "can't find the time..." to do anything, please remember that dying intestate (without a will) is the most precarious position of all—without instructions to the contrary, the state laws of natural lineage will prevail. This means that you lose control of where your assets go, who raises your children, who your executor will be, and how your possessions will be disbursed. You are giving tacit permission for your relatives to get together (at your expense) and argue over who inherits the jewelry, the antique sewing machine, the china, and even the minor children (who may become very attractive assets because of the insurance policy naming them principal beneficiaries).

Remember, there are no simple answers to these complex issues. Most of my clients express the desire for simple will and simple estate planning. This chapter just the *foundation* for simple estate planning.

My experience, as uncommon as it may seem, irrevocably changed two young lives. Sadly, my parents felt that their estate planning *was* prudent. Their ignorance, hopefully, will serve as a warning to each reader.

If you can't take it with you, at least you ought to be able to decide who gets it after you are gone.

# chapter fourteen

# A Short Course In Finance And Insuranese

---

### Annual Percentage Rate

The rate of interest charged by a lender, expressed as the monthly interest times 12 (months). It does *not* take into account compounding, which increases the actual amount of interest charged on an unpaid monthly balance.

### Annual Renewal Term Life Insurance

Term life insurance which costs more each and every year for the same amount of coverage because you are paying only for one year of mortality at a time. Most beneficial when a small period of insurance is needed.

### Annuity

An investment vehicle that accumulates money tax-deferred until it is withdrawn—there are surrender charges in the early years for total withdrawal and an early distribution penalty for withdrawal before the age of 59 1/2.

This is a long-term investment only—once it is annuitized it becomes a fixed income vehicle with equal monthly payments (in various payment options) for a specified number of years.

## Appreciable Asset

Something purchased which is expected to increase in value over time (house, collectibles, stocks, bonds, etc.)

## Beneficiary

The person(s) named in a life insurance policy to receive the death benefit—there are *primary* or first beneficiaries and *contingent* beneficiaries or "second-in-line" beneficiaries.

## Boilerplate

Standard clauses or agreements that can be run off on a printer, they do not take into account the unique situation of a client or go into great detail;

## Cash Value

Technically known as "cash surrender value," this is the amount of money or savings within your life insurance policy that can be borrowed back from the insurance company. The cash value is invested by the insurance company and grows in value as you add to it (paying premiums) and investment earnings are credited to it.

However, you cannot borrow your savings from these policies without reducing your death benefit amount.

## Certificate of Deposit (CD)

A contract issued by a bank or other lending institution that guarantees you a specific locked-in interest rate for a period of time. Generally, the longer the time you allow the institution to use your money, the higher the interest rate. Savings & Loans will usually offer a higher interest rate than a commercial bank.

## Certified Financial Planner

A person who has completed the required course work from the College of Financial Planning is permitted to use the trademarked CFP (Certified Financial Planner) designation. CFPs are regulated by the International Board of Standards and Practices for Certified Financial Planners.

## Co-Insurance

The amount of out-of-pocket money an insured must contribute before the insurance will pay 100% of the costs of covered losses—after the policy deductible is satisfied, most insurance companies require an insured to bear a specified percentage of covered expenses.

## Common Disaster

When an insured and a spouse both die simultaneously in an accident or disaster and it is difficult or impossible to tell which one may have died first.

## Compound Interest

Generally provides the greatest profit over time. Each time interest is calculated, it is figured on the entire amount, including the principal *and interest from the* last *calculation*. Example: Nine months of interest on a $1,000 investment paying 8.75% and compounded quarterly is $67.00. The same rate of return at simple interest would yield only $65.63.

## Consumer Debt

Debt from credit on purchases that are not considered investments, savings, mortgage payments or other items which have greater future potential of dollar value.

## Consumer Debt Ratio

The proportion of take-home pay that is going to consumer debt, such as car payments, credit cards, and other time payments or installment loans.This does *not* include mortgage payments or home equity loans.

## Contingent Beneficiary

The second beneficiary(ies) on an insurance policy who receive(s) the death proceeds only if the primary beneficiary(ies) is/are not living.

## Convertible Term Insurance

A policy that starts out as term insurance but can be changed to a cash value policy to accumulate savings.

When this conversion is made, the premium necessary to pay for an equal amount of death benefit will jump significantly.

## Cost of Money

Varies over time. Usually costs depend on market competition between those who are either advertising for your dollars or what the market will bear. The greater the number of those asking for money and the smaller the number of lenders, the greater the price to borrow that money. There are "sales" on money from time to time— higher interest rates paid to you or lower interest rates charged to you.

## Credit

Committing future expected income for a purpose today. Money is a commodity that is bought and sold just like any other tangible item. Costs vary and increase according to how long it is wanted and the perceived risk of the lender.

## Credit Life or Mortgage Insurance

Decreasing term life insurance which is commonly sold by lenders for a death benefit on a home, car or other item bought on payments, with one dangerous difference: The beneficiary is not someone you name; it is the creditor. The death benefit decreases each year but the premium remains the same. At the end of the term of the policy, the death benefit reduces to zero.

Most of us would like to hand over our house free and clear to our family if we die, but not at the expense of food on the table and the cash needed for utilities, clothing, medical needs, school tuition, etc. Your spouse should make the final decision—whether to pay off a home mortgage when you die or to continue making payments while using your death insurance for daily survival.

## Debt

May be considered good or bad, depending on the situation, Always look through the options whether to pay cash or to buy on credit and string out the number of payments. Whenever you give away cash, you are losing the opportunity cost of what that money would have done if it had been working for you over a period of time.

## Decreasing Term Insurance

Term life insurance with a level premium and a decreasing death benefit over the term of the policy. This is the most expensive type of term insurance because even though the premium remains the same, the amount of death benefit keeps decreasing. This is heavily sold by lenders to cover a home mortgage loan in case of the premature death of the insured (also known as *credit life insurance*).

## "Deep Pockets Theory"

A way to measure the attractiveness of someone when considering a suit against them—the greater their assets or earning power (their "deep pockets" of money), the more likely they will be sued for a larger amount of damages in the case of an injury or other liability claim against them.

## Depreciable Asset

An asset that is expected to decrease in value over time (most cars, stereos, furniture, etc.)

## Disposable Income

That income that provides for your daily living activities and survival and is spent for items which do not appreciate or provide any long-term benefits.g., food, utilities, car payments, insurance premiums, vacations, entertaiunment, household expenses, etc.

## Fiduciary

A person occupying a position of trust or responsibility to perform a specified duty, such as an executor, administrator or trustee.

## Financial Planner

Lacking any further appellation (Certified Financial Planner, Registered Financial Planner, or Chartered

Financial Consultant), it means virtually nothing—any salesperson can say he or she is a "financial planner," even though he or she has had no special training, adheres to no special set of rules, and is not regulated by any association.

### Gross Income

Income before federal, state, local and Social Security taxes are withheld (pre-tax income)—*not* the money you have to manage. It is misleading to use this term for financial planning purposes.

### Inflation

Inflation is a silent but deadly money killer to long-term goals, as it forces one to pay higher and higher prices for goods and services which, in turn, decreases the buying power of both individuals and business.

Business passes on the increased costs of inflation by raising prices for its products to consumers. But consumers—us—suffer a real loss of money when prices escalate at a faster rate than income (paychecks) rise. Long-term investments must continually attempt to beat the erosion of inflation.

### Intestate

When a person dies without a will and his property is distributed according to the laws of the state in which he lived and in which he owned property, which may bear little or no resemblance to what the deceased may have wanted.

### IRA (Individual Retirement Account)

A tax label you "stamp" on a wide variety of investment vehicles to tell Uncle Sam not to tax them before retirement—CDs, Money Market mutual funds, conservative mutual funds, aggressive growth mutual funds, insurance annuities, stocks, bonds, even gold coins minted by the U.S. Government can all be part of your IRA.

## Joint and Survivor Account

An account set up with more than one name which becomes payable directly to the surviving owner(s) in case of the death of one of the owners of the account.

## Joint and Survivor Annuity

An agreement with an annuity company or plan whereby payments are made to one annuitant and upon that person's death, continue to the survivor designated on the original contract. These are commonly used with pension plans, insurance annuities, or insurance death benefit settlements.

## Joint Tenants With Rights of Survivorship (JTWROS)

Both persons designated as owners of a security or other tangible property wholly own the property individually as well as jointly. In the case of investments, this means one owner may not dispose of that property without the permission of the other owner. For estate planning purposes, it means that if one owner dies, the property passes *outside* of the will, directly to the surviving owner.

## Level Term Life Insurance

A type of term insurance with a level term death benefit at a level premium for a stated period of time—5, 10, 15, even 20 years—after which the premium increases for the next stated period. It is usually guaranteed renewable. If you have a growing family, you should purchase the longest period you can find with competitive rates. If you then reduce the amount of death coverage at each renewal (as your need for death protection decreases over the years), it can remain affordable over the long run.

## Long-Term Interest

The rate of return on longer-term money vehicles such as mutual funds, 30-year Treasury bonds, etc., During much of 1989 and 1990, short-term interest has been even higher than longer-term rates, which is contrary to the normal yield time curve. Usually someone has to pay you more to get your money for a longer period of time.

## Money Market (Bank) Demand Account

A higher-performing bank account than a regular passbook savings account. Interest rates are better but not as high as a money market mutual fund (see below). This is a relatively new instrument banks developed to compete with other vehicles. This type of account is also insured by the FDIC.

## Money Market Mutual Fund

A specific type of mutual fund which attempts to be managed at $1.00 per share, it contains short-term money instruments such as Treasury bills, commercial paper, and other low-risk instruments.

Although these are not guaranteed, many of the vehicles are instruments issued by the U.S. Government. Interest rates change daily. Checkwriting privileges can be requested, giving you instant access to the total account.

Seek a Money Market fund with no distribution charges, which could lower your interest rate by $1/2$% or more.

Do not automatically choose the highest paying Money Market—they may be taking greater risks with your principal or reducing management fees which they expect to reclaim later through lower interest rates.

Money Markets are a good place for short-term money storage or short-term goals such as an emergency fund. You generally must deposit a minimum of $1,000 to open an account.

## Mortgage Insurance (see Credit Life Insurance, Decreasing Term Insurance)

## Net Income

The income remaining *after* federal, state, local, and Social Security taxes have been withheld and all pre-tax contributions to employer plans have been withheld, it can be considered as take-home pay for general financial planning purposes.

## Opportunity Cost

The opportunity for return on your money that is lost by choosing one investment over another—e.g., the interest lost by putting your savings in a passbook bank account rather than a higher-yielding CD or mutual fund. The opportunity cost of choosing one option is the loss of the ability to make other choices.

## OPM (Other People's Money)

Utilizing money either without being charged for borrowing (e.g., by paying off the total balance on a credit card each month) or using money at a lower cost than you will gain from investing it somewhere else (e.g., taking out a second mortgage at 10% a year to fund a business from which you expect to net 50%). This concept usually involves leveraging a smaller amount of borrowed money to fund a larger investment vehicle.

## POD (Payable on Demand) Account

An account into which an individual deposits funds payable to a beneficiary at the death of the owner—the owner maintains complete control of the account (including any withdrawals) during his or her lifetime.

## Point of Sale (POS)

Interest on credit purchases may be calculated from the moment an item is bought (the point of sale) and not from the closing date or grace period of 25 to 30 days after the sale. Point of sale credit arrangements look attractive until you realize you will never be using OPM (Other People's Money) free for even one day.

## Price

Determined by negotiation between a buyer and a seller, price may have little to do with value. Price only indicates what the consumer market will bear.

## Primary Beneficiary

The first beneficiary(ies) on a life insurance policy to receive the death benefit if the insured dies; if the first beneficiary does not survive the insured, his or her heirs do not inherit the death benefit—the money passes to the second or contingent beneficiary.

## Registered Financial Planner

A person who has applied and been accepted by the Registry of Financial Planning Practitioners after rigorous examination and submission of evidence that the practitioner's primary vocation is financial planning and that he or she will follow the required comprehensive planning process.

## Risk Management

Methods of managing risk such as risk avoidance, risk reduction, risk retention (self-insuring) and risk transfer (the use of insurance); usually the best kind of risk management is a combination of all of the above.

## Rule of 72

A simple formula to roughly determine how fast money will grow under compound interest. Just divide the number 72 by a rate of return; the answer reveals how many years it will take to double your money. This formula can also show how fast inflation will eat up your present dollars in the future.

## Seed Dollars

The most valuable of all dollars because they come from your effort or employment. Seed dollars can be saved and produce investment dollars over time or spent for immediate expenses—the more seed dollars you save and invest, the more dollars you will earn on them.

## Self-Defense Risk Management

Using insurance wisely—transferring the largest risks to the insurance company while retaining the smaller risks and working the extra money for your own benefit; the optimum mix between premium dollars and benefits to achieve the greatest value for your premium dollar.

## Seven Day CD

A new vehicle marketed by banks to offset the large amounts of money that have been flowing into money market mutual funds. The bank offers a guaranteed interest rate for seven days. After each seven-day period, they can change the interest rate, and you must make a new decision whether to allow them to keep your money for another seven days.

Some banks play a game, advertising initial high rates with no intention of staying competitive later; after consumers deposit their money, the banks slowly reduce their rates. Many consumers do not watch their money closely and do not know this is happening. Check with your institution every three or four weeks and continue to compare your bank's seven-day rate with other banks—you owe it to the banks who give you a competitive return to do business with them.

## Short-Term Interest

The rate of return or interest collected on short-term vehicles, such as savings accounts, Treasury bills, seven-day CDs, money market bank accounts, or money market mutual funds. These are considered to low-risk investment vehicles and, consequently, offer a lower yield to compensate for the relative safety of the principal. These vehicles are good for short-term goals, such as an emergency fund, or financial goals you need to reach within two years.

## Simple Interest

A method of figuring interest that results in the lowest amount of profit gained over time, calculated by taking the quoted interest rate and dividing it by the number of months of the deposit. Example: $1,000 at 8.75% for 9 months = 8.75% divided by 12 months (.730) x 9 months = 6.56% profit or a total of $1,065 (or $65.56 profit). Compare the result if the same amount is figured using compound interest.

## Single Premium Life Insurance

A type of whole life insurance in which you prepay your entire insurance premium...forever. Do not confuse this with *Single Pay life,* which only prepays premiums for a certain period of time, after which money may need to be added if interest rate projections do not match those you were shown.

If you understand the time value of money and what your precious seed dollars could be doing for you if you were working them instead of the insurance company, you may well opt for other types of insurance.

## Stop-Loss Limit

The amount of out-of-pocket money you must pay on a health insurance claim before the insurance company begins to pay 100% of covered expenses, which occurs after the deductible is paid and any co-insurance payments are made for eligible expenses.

## Sweat Equity

Financial progress and money accumulation from the sweat of your own labor, such as purchasing an older home and remodeling it before reselling it.

## Tax-Deductible

Any vehicle in which the contribution or the interest earned on it is partially or fully deductible from federal and/or state taxes.

## Tax-Deferred

The profits from this type of investment are taxed some time in the future, not when they are actually made.

## Tax-Exempt

An investment whose profits are never taxed, even in the future—e.g., municipal bonds. Whether or not this type of investment is right for you depends upon your marginal (or highest dollar) tax bracket because the return on any tax exempt vehicle will be much lower than on a similar taxable investment. Both federal and state income taxes should be considered when examining taxable vs. tax-exempt investments.

## Tax Shelter

An investment that becomes more attractive because it carries with it some form of tax advantage—tax-deferred, tax deductible, or tax-exempt—which makes the investment return more attractive and more favorable. There is usually a lower rate of return on this type of investment due to the added tax advantage.

## Term Insurance

A policy that lasts for a specific time period—one year, 5, 10, even 20—after which it can be automatically renewed without evidence of insurability, usually until age 70 or even later. It pays only if you die while you own the policy. It costs more for each renewal period.

## Totten Trust

A trust in which you deposit funds and over which you maintain total control during your lifetime. When you die, however, the trust is paid to the beneficiary you have named in it.

## Universal Life Insurance

A hybrid policy that is a form of cash value insurance with flexible premiums and a different format (or, if you prefer, annual term insurance with a savings feature added). This kind of insurance policy can be deceiving if you do not understand that you are actually purchasing a policy with a lower guarantee and with nothing more than *projections* of earnings on your cash value. The interest rates projected are not guarantees, though you can find what they really are guaranteeing if you search through enough fine print—some companies pay only 4% on the first $1,000 cash value and interest at whatever rates it feels like declaring on the rest of your savings.

If premiums on this type of policy seem lower than those on term insurance policies you've researched, it's because the premium you have been quoted may *not* be what is required to maintain the policy in force for the total period of coverage stated in the policy. If your planned premium is less than that required to maintain the death benefit, your monthly premiums are taken from your savings or cash value account. It is possible for this kind of policy to run out of money in your cash accumuation account if the rates of return you were originally promised do not materialize year after year.

## Variable Life Insurance

Similar to whole life or universal life policies, except that your savings inside it are dependent on the investment experience of an underlying separate account. Any extra earnings from the savings account are added to your death benefit. Instead of transferring the risk of your savings to the insurance company, you have held onto it!

Some variable policies designate a guaranteed death amount regardless of the investment experience of your savings; others guarantee the death benefit only for a short period of years if the investment does not perform well.

It is highly questionable whether you want your death benefit dependent on an investment inside your insurance policy. When your purchase death protection, you should, by paying the premium, be transferring the risk.

## Whole Life Insurance

A policy that maintains a level death benefit by combining decreasing term insurance with an increasing savings portion called the cash surrender value. The premium is averaged over your lifetime, costing you more before age 65 so you can pay less after you retire. A portion of each premium payment goes to the term insurance, another portion to your savings inside the policy.

Since you usually get only the death benefit if you die, the "savings" revert back to the company. If you take your savings from the policy, you lose your death protection. You can borrow money from the insurance company—usually up to 90% of the cash value at current interest

ates. You are charged interest on these borrowings until
ou pay back all interest and the outstanding loan. At the
ame time, your death protection is reduced to match the
•an—dollar for dollar.

## early Renewable Term Insurance

Term insurance that is automatically renewed each
ear, with an accompanying premium rate increase or
tep-rate increase for the same amount of coverage. Its
remiums are based on the age of the insured during each
ear of the policy, which is why they go up each year on
1e insured's birthday. This type of coverage is best uti-
zed when only a short period of coverage—3 years or less
-is desired.

## afterword

# You're Ready
# For Battle!

You're now ready to outrun every adversary, outwit every foe, and protect your money at least as well as the large institutions and corporations panting for it. This book *should* have made you more skeptical—blind trust is a poor foundation on which to build any long-term business relationship.

Remember: Information is more powerful and more important than money itself.

Subscribe to the KISS Theory (Keep it Simple Stupid) whenever you meet those whose sophistication seemingly outstrips yours.

You will face innumerable glittering "dog and pony shows" from salespeople intent on separating you from your money. Do not be deceived or falsely impressed by the trappings of credibility, wealth or competence. Most of the people you meet probably know less about *their* money than you now do about *yours*.

There are many excellent books out there that will help you explore and understand specific vehicles that could not be discussed in great detail in this short primer. Visit your library and/or bookstore and read, read, read.

Play the Money Game well. Your family and your future are depending on it.

| index |

# Get Rich Slow